"My God, my God, why have you forsaken me?"

MARK 15:34

FAITH
STRIPPED
to its ESSENCE

A Discordant Pilgrimage
through Shūsaku Endō's *Silence*

PATRICK T. REARDON

FAITH STRIPPED TO ITS ESSENCE
A Discordant Pilgrimage Through Shusaku Endo's *Silence*
Patrick T. Reardon

Edited by Gregory F.A. Pierce
Cover and text design by Patricia A. Lynch
Cover image © Jacky Brown, under license from Bigstock

Published by ACTA Publications, 4848 N. Clark St.,
Chicago, IL 60640, (800) 397-2282, actapublications.com

Library of Congress Catalog Number: 2016951835
ISBN: 978-0-87946-581-0
Printed in the United States of America by Total Printing Systems
Year 25 24 23 22 21 20 19 18 17 16
Printing 12 11 10 9 8 7 6 5 4 3 2

♻ Text printed on 30% post-consumer recycled paper

CONTENTS

Dedicated to Sarah, Tara, and David Joseph
and, as always, to Cathy

In memory of David Michael Reardon

Thanks to Greg Pierce, Thomas Pace, Patricia Cloud,
Julie Coplon, and Joan Servatius.

INTRODUCTION

There is a mystery at the heart of Shusaku Endo's 1966 novel *Silence*, and it is this: Father Sebastian Rodrigues, a seventeenth-century Jesuit priest from Portugal, steals into Japan during a time of terror-filled, bloody repressions of Christianity in which hundreds of believers in Jesus are routinely tortured and executed. He lives in hiding, providing the sacraments when and where he can to communities of Christians who, at great peril, have kept their faith alive in secret. As one of the few priests still in Japan, he is a symbol of the Church, a beacon and a model for those who come to him for spiritual solace and support. Yet, in the end, he goes against all that he has stood for.

In the end, psychologically assaulted by his captors, shaken to his core by the sounds of Christians moaning over the torture pit just a short distance away, he goes through a Japanese ceremony for rejecting his faith. To show his rejection of his beliefs, he ritually steps on — "tramples" — a worn, wooden image of Jesus, a *fumi-e*.

He does this not to save himself from physical torture, but because he has been told that, unless he apostatizes, the Christians he can hear moaning in a nearby torture chamber will suffer more and will die, and will be followed by others.

For other Christians, particularly his religious superiors back in Europe, this act is a violation of his faith. It is a betrayal.

Yet, during the next three decades until his death, when Rodrigues is being held under house arrest and writes, as he is ordered, a book disavowing Christianity, he refuses to see himself as a betrayer.

"Lord," he says in prayer, "you alone know that I did not renounce my faith."

This is the mystery. Is Rodrigues deceiving himself? Is he wildly deluded about what he has done and what it means? Is he a craven coward who cannot even face — or does not even realize — the consequences of his actions?

Or is he right?

Is there some way that, in rejecting his faith — in trampling on the image of Jesus — Rodrigues has mined a deeper faith?

Is he right when he says that he did what Jesus would have done? Or is he kidding himself?

Silence is a novel about the meaning of faith and the expression of faith. It is also the basis of the motion picture directed by Martin Scorsese.

Both the novel and the movie offer a doorway for individuals and groups to enter into the questions Endo raises about the world then and our world now, about Catholicism, Christianity, and all the various religious belief systems and about how they relate to one another.

What are we required to do because of our faith? What does it mean to believe?

Silence is a novel filled with a cacophony of voices arguing and agonizing about faith. Rodrigues is the central character of the book, but there are many others — his colleague Father Francis Garrpe, his teacher and fellow apostate Father Christovao Ferreira, the Japanese Christians these priests came to serve, the Judas-like Kichijiro, and Inoue, the clever, Christian-trained official leading the persecutions.

In this pilgrimage through the discordant voices of faith in Endo's novel, there are chapters devoted to each of the main characters and their own experience of belief. And there are several chapters that center on Rodrigues. These characters are all believers in one way or another, but they are far from unified in their approach. Just as we are.

Some stories from *Silence* are recorded several times here, each time from the perspective of a different character. In a way, this commentary takes the novel apart and puts it back together again in order to highlight the distinctly different answers that its characters arrive at when faced with the question of faith.

Faith in *Silence* is a life-and-death question.

What is required by faith? What does it mean to believe? What are the costs?

Is Rodrigues a sinner?

Or a saint?

Patrick T. Reardon
Chicago, Illinois

AUTHOR'S NOTE

Each of the twelve chapters in this book ends with a set of questions. These are not extraneous. Rather, they are an extension of each chapter's theme and presentation.

Endo's *Silence* is a novel of questions. Knotty, painful questions that Father Sebastian Rodrigues must face, and knotty questions that the story raises for every reader.

These end-of-chapter questions are integral to my commentary on the novel, integral to this pilgrimage through *Silence*. They are all implicit in the story that Endo has written — and in the life of belief that each human being is called to lead.

These questions are offered for use in personal reflection and in group discussion. They are reminders that *Silence* isn't only a story about Rodrigues. It is also our story, and the questions about faith that the novel raises are our questions. These are questions we have to face in our own lives, questions about what has meaning for us and what faith requires of us.

In *Silence*, Rodrigues, Francis Garrpe, and Christovao Ferreira are Catholic missionaries in Japan. The Japanese people who have been baptized by them and by other European priests are Catholics as well.

Nonetheless, Shusaku Endo refers to them by the more general term as "Christians."

He does this, I think, for two reasons.

First, he wants to emphasize the sharp cultural differences between Europe and Japan as embodied in religious faith. In the novel, Christianity is seen as an expression of the European world and mind-set that is alien to the Japanese way of life and way of thinking. For Endo, the important fact isn't that Rodrigues and the others are Catholics, rather than Lutherans, for example, but that they are European Christians rather than Japanese Buddhists.

Second, the central question for Rodrigues is this: What would Jesus do? By using the term "Christians" throughout *Silence*, Endo is emphasizing the connection between the faith proclaimed by the priests and the Christ whose teaching is the basis of that faith.

In deference to Endo, I use the term "Christian" rather than "Catholic" in my examination of and commentary on *Silence* in the following pages.

It is also worth noting that Endo is often careless in the minor details of his storytelling.

Numbers, for instance, don't always match, such as the number of Christians who are ordered to apostatize in the prison before the one-eyed man is killed. Similarly, the details of the life of Father Christovao Ferreira in Japan and Portugal as laid out in the novel don't quite mesh, and some aspects of the torture in the pit, as Endo describes them, seem to be incomplete or, at least, unclear.

In the following pages, I have chosen, for the most part, not to point out such discrepancies.

PART ONE
FAITH

"Where were you when I laid the foundation of the earth?
Tell me, if you have understanding,
Who determined its measurements — surely you know!
Or who stretched the line upon it?
On what were its bases sunk,
or who laid its cornerstone
when the morning stars sang together
and all the heavenly beings shouted for joy?"

JOB 38:4-7

CHAPTER ONE
THE FAITH OF FATHER FRANCIS GARRPE

Father Sebastian Rodrigues is not alone when he is smuggled into Japan in the face of religious persecution and ultimately is pushed to the psychic limit at the edge of the torture pit. With him is another Jesuit missionary, Father Francis Garrpe, who confronts many of the same terrors and threats.

Nearly all of *Silence* is presented in Rodrigues' words and from his point of view. Shusaku Endo puts the reader inside the heart and mind of the priest as he struggles to live out his Christian beliefs and ideals. The result is a richly nuanced portrait of a man who is forced to confront the meaning of his life.

By contrast, Garrpe's personality, faith, and trials are sketched with a few quick brushstrokes. Yet, in sharing the same travails, Garrpe provides a clear-cut counterpoint to Rodrigues.

As Endo spells out early in the novel, the two men are friends and former classmates at the Jesuit seminary in the ancient Campolide monastery outside of Lisbon. It was there that they were taught theology by Father Christovao Ferreira, a veteran missionary and a man they greatly admired. Ferreira was an imposing figure known for his "gentle charity," a tall man with a full chestnut beard that gave him "an air of kindness combined with gravity." His clear blue eyes, slightly hollowed, were set in a face that seemed to glow with "soft radiant light."

Now, though, reports have been received that, under threat of torture, Ferreira, known for his "indomitable courage," has denied the Christian faith and become an apostate.

Rodrigues and Garrpe as well as a friend and former classmate, Father Juan de Santa Maria, cannot understand why their revered teacher would abase himself before his persecutors rather than accept "a glorious martyrdom."

So, even though they are only in their late twenties or early thirties, they propose to their superiors that they sail for Japan, smuggle themselves into the country, and find out the truth about Ferreira. When they obtain grudging approval, the priests sail east and more than a year later finally arrive in May of 1639 in the Portuguese-controlled city of Macao on the coast of China, across from Hong Kong.

"Sheep without a shepherd"

In Macao, however, the Jesuit rector Father Valignano initially refuses to permit them to cross to Japan, insisting that it is too dangerous. The three, especially Garrpe, respond with eloquent arguments about the need for them to risk their lives in the face of terrible persecution. As Santa Marta tells the rector, the mission isn't only to find out what happened to Ferreira: "In that stricken land, the Christians have lost their priests and are like a flock of sheep without a shepherd."

Valignano is swayed, but only Garrpe and Rodrigues are able to go. Wracked by fevers, Santa Marta is very sick, completely worn out by their arduous journey and a case of malaria. He stays behind and, as Rodrigues notes in a letter to his superiors in Portugal, is likely to be able to live a safe and happy life while his friends suffer at the hands of pagans.

Before Rodrigues and Garrpe sail, they find a Japanese peasant in his late twenties named Kichijiro who is willing to lead them to a Christian community near Nagasaki, but he is far from an ideal guide. A drunken fisherman with a crafty look in his eyes, he staggers into the room to meet them, dressed in rags.

During the meeting and in later scenes, Garrpe shows himself to be a question-asker and someone who is prone to emotional outbursts.

With Kichijiro, Garrpe takes the role of an interrogator, insistently demanding with increasing bitterness again and again that the man say if he is a Christian. But, despite describing the torture of twenty-four Christians on the island of Kyushu near Nagasaki, Kichijiro won't answer Garrpe's question. Later, the Jesuit continues his interrogation but again gets no response. Clearly exasperated, Garrpe even asks the man if he is Japanese. No answer.

When the two priests finally are taken in a small boat on a dark night to the Japanese mainland, Kichijiro is the first to wade ashore. The two Jesuits are left in the shadows by the water, and when they hear the sounds of a passing woman, the danger of their situation hits them.

With tears in his eyes, Garrpe tells Rodrigues that "the weak-minded coward" will never come back. They've been abandoned. He even quotes from the story of Jesus in the Garden of Gethsemane: "A band of soldiers went there with lanterns and torches and weapons."

Soon, though, a group of Christians from the village of Tomogi emerge out of the dark. Kichijiro is with them.

The Jesuits are hidden in a charcoal hut on a hill above the village, and, when some Christians come to visit, Garrpe again is asking questions, this time about what has been happening in the Christian community in the six years since they've had a priest to serve them. Later, when two women bring food, they giggle as they watch the men eat, prompting an angry Garrpe to ask, "Are we so queer? Is our way of eating so funny?"

Rodrigues and Garrpe are under intense stress. For their protection and the protection of the village, the two priests are cooped up in the hut throughout each long day and only see their flock at night when the believers are able to furtively make their way up the hill through the trees. Rodrigues and Garrpe know that they could be discovered at any moment by Japanese officials who will torture them. They spend their long days in a kind of terrified boredom, picking at the lice that infest their bodies.

One day, the two young men have had enough, and joyfully, boyish-ly, they step out of the hut into the sunlight and fresh air where they take off their kimonos and let the sun wash over them. This becomes a daily routine, and Garrpe is filled with happiness, nicknaming the hut their "monastery" and relishing their walks through the woods.

Then, to their shock, they're spotted by two men, and they fear they've endangered themselves and their flock. That night, someone is at the door of their hut. "Padre, Padre," a voice whispers. Rodrigues goes to open the door, but Garrpe calls him an "idiot" and tells him to stop.

Rodrigues opens the door anyway, and the men outside, the ones who spotted them in the woods, turn out to be emissaries from the Christian community on the island of Fukazawa in the Goto Islands, about sixty miles away.

The men ask for one of the priests to come and minister to their town. After consulting with the fearful Christians from Tomogi, Rodrigues goes to Fukazawa for a five-day visit while Garrpe stays behind.

Although Rodrigues comes back as scheduled, the two Jesuits are soon forced to go their separate ways.

"Lord, hear our prayer!"

In two successive raids, soldiers and samurai, tipped off by an informer, scour the village for evidence of Christianity and take four hostages. Later, from hiding, Rodrigues and Garrpe learn how two of the four are martyred. Rather than remain hiding in their hut (and endangering the village even more), the priests resolve to go out, each in his own direction, to find other Christians to serve, regardless of the risk. And so they part.

It is not until Rodrigues has been captured and held in prison that he sees Garrpe again.

It is a horrific moment.

Rodrigues has been taken out of the prison and brought to a pine grove with a view of a nearby beach. He is told to sit on a stool and wait. As he does, a man he knows only as the interpreter begins to gleefully taunt him. He tells Rodrigues that he will soon have a chance to see Garrpe once again.

In the distance, the Jesuit sees a group of prisoners being walked up the gray beach. In front, bound together in chains, are three Christians, one of whom is a woman he knows as Monica. Behind them is Garrpe.

On the beach, the guards begin to wrap in three prisoners tightly in straw mats, covering their whole bodies except their heads and feet in a way that makes them look like "basket worms." They are awkward and virtually immobile.

The interpreter explains to Rodrigues that the officials on the beach are telling Garrpe that he has a choice to make. If he rejects his Christian beliefs and "tramples" on the *fumi-e*, an image of Jesus, the three prisoners will be spared. But, if he does not apostatize, they will be killed.

The three prisoners have already rejected Christianity and ritually stepped on the *fumi-e*, but they're not important, the interpreter says. The Japanese officials only hound such Christian lay people in order to get the priests themselves to turn their backs on their faith.

Silently, inside his head, Rodrigues shouts to Garrpe, "Apostatize! Apostatize!" But he says nothing out loud.

On the beach, Monica and the two others have been loaded into the boat, and the boat is moving into deeper water.

Garrpe is being forced to choose.

Suddenly, as Rodrigues watches, the priest runs into the surf and swims toward the boat, shouting, "Lord, hear our prayer!"

Garrpe's head rises and falls in the waves, and each time it comes above the water surface Rodrigues can hear, "Lord, hear our prayer!" Garrpe's head looks "like a piece of black dust" on the waves.

Now, in the boat, one of the guards takes a lance and pushes the first of the Christian prisoners into the water, then the second, then Monica. They sink quickly under the waves.

Only Garrpe's head remains above the surface of the sea.

And then that too is gone.

"At least Garrpe was clean," the interpreter tells Rodrigues. "But you...you...you are the most weak-willed. You don't deserve the name 'father.'"

Questions for Reflection or Discussion

Why does Garrpe ask so many questions of others? Do you every find yourself doing the same thing? Why?

Garrpe calls Kichijiro a "weak-minded coward." He calls Rodrigues an "idiot" when his friend goes to open the door to their hut. Do you ever use insults and name-calling to make a point? Is it effective? Give some examples.

Garrpe dives into the sea and swims to the boat holding the three Christians tied up in straw mats like "basket worms"? What do you think he hopes to accomplish? Does it work? Why or why not?

Garrpe shouts, "Lord, hear our prayer," over and over and over as he swims. Do you think he, like Rodrigues, feels betrayed because he believes God has remained silent in the face of such persecution? Have you felt betrayed by God? Explain your answer.

How would you describe Garrpe's faith? In what ways is it similar or different from your own?

CHAPTER TWO
THE FAITH OF JAPANESE CHRISTIANS

Running like a river of blood through *Silence* are the stories of Japanese Christians who, for their faith, suffer great torments and death at the hands of shogunate officials.

Again and again, Shusaku Endo tells of the many ways they demonstrate a love and reverence for Christianity that is simple, direct, and total. Despite great dangers, they build their lives around the secret living out of their beliefs, praying together in hidden gatherings in the midst of a society that sees them as violators of the Japanese culture.

When discovered and put to the test, they endure, and they die.

Japanese leaders initially welcomed missionary priests, Endo notes, but that all changed when Toyotomi Hideyoshi, the imperial regent, launched a brutal campaign against the religion, seeking to eradicate Christianity from the nation's culture and from its soil. The first page of *Silence* tells of twenty-six priests and lay people who were the initial martyrs in the persecution, followed by the torture and execution of Christians from one end of Japan to the other. On a single day in one location, as many as seventy believers were martyred for their faith.

In 1614, the Shogun Tokugawa Ieyasu ordered all missionaries out of Japan. But rather than leave their flocks without shepherds, thirty-seven priests, including Father Christovao Ferreira, decided to go into hiding. (The novel implies but doesn't state that, at some point in the next twenty years, Ferreira returned for a time to Portugal where he served as the seminary teacher of Father Sebastian Rodrigues and Father Francis Garrpe before going back to Japan.)

Endo writes that Ferreira had sent a letter back to his superiors in 1632, in which he described the agonies of five priests (four Jesuits and one Franciscan) and two women. The local magistrate, wanting to force them to renounce Christianity, ordered that they be viciously tortured but kept alive. The seven were taken to the sulphur springs of volcanic Mount Unzen where, in the cold weather, they could see the steam rising from the boiling lake. Each was stripped and bound to a post at the edge of the lake, and ladles full of scalding water were poured over their bodies.

In his letter, Ferreira called them "heroes of Christ." The younger of the two women collapsed and was taken away, but each of the remaining victims was tortured as many as six times over a thirty-three-day period.

Finally, Ferreira wrote with pride, the magistrate realized "that all the springs in Unzen would run dry" before the victims would repudiate their beliefs. He put the priests in prison and sent the woman to a brothel. "This whole struggle," Ferreira wrote triumphantly, "has had the effect of spreading our doctrine among the multitude and strengthening the faith of our Christians."

"Trample!"

But, now, it is seven years later.

Many more priests and lay people have died, and word has reached Europe that Ferreira himself may have abandoned the faith. Rodrigues and Garrpe have landed near Nagasaki and have been taken by a group of Christians to a small shack on a hill above their village named Tomogi. The two men realize that they may be the only priests still active anywhere in Japan.

When the Christians of Tomogi tell the Jesuits they haven't seen a priest in six years, Garrpe asks how they have been able to keep alive the faith.

The Christians explain that, in the absence of missionaries, they had organized themselves. One of the older men, Jiisama, was given the role of priest, and it was his job to baptize the children. A group of men had the task of teaching the faith to the others and leading them in prayer.

Such activities carried a deadly threat if discovered by the authorities. Even so, the lay leaders developed a secret calendar of church feasts so that Easter and Christmas could be celebrated at the right time in the year. When they gathered to pray, a holy picture was set up as if on an altar. They said the Our Father and Hail Mary and other prayers in Latin, as they had been taught long ago by the missionaries.

Now, with Rodrigues and Garrpe in their midst, the Christians are overjoyed. After being led up the hill to their hut, the priests take the crucifixes from around their necks and give them to their two guides. The faces of the men fill with happiness, and they bow low to the ground and press the crucifixes to their foreheads.

For about a month, Endo writes, the two priests are able to minister to their new flock. Then, in a noonday raid, several samurai and guards sweep down on Tomogi, searching the village from end to end for any evidence of Christianity. Finding none, they demand that the peasants acknowledge their adherence to the banned religion or they will take a hostage.

"An informer recently told us that amongst you that there are secret adherents of this forbidden Christian sect," a samurai says. A bribe of 100 pieces of silver is offered to anyone who will reveal the truth.

Jiisama tells the leader that Tomogi is a law-abiding village, but the leading samurai won't hear it. He orders Jiisama to be bound in ropes and taken away. Later, the village is forced to come up with three more hostages. Kichijiro, the drunken guide of the two priests, is pressured into going, and two village men, Mokichi and the aged Ichizo, volunteer to join him.

Before they go, Mokichi asks the Jesuits, "Father, if we are ordered to trample on the *fumi-e*...if we don't trample, everyone in the village will be cross-examined. What are we to do?"

Impulsively, Rodrigues tells them, "Trample! Trample!" as Garrpe silently reproaches him.

And so they do. When the three are brought before officials for a trial, each places his foot as ordered on an image of the Virgin Mary and the Christ Child — first, Kichijiro, then Mokichi and Ichizo. But the officials notice how difficult it is for at least two of them, so the three are given a new test: to spit on the crucifix and to call Mary a whore.

Ichizo tries to spit, but can't. Neither can Mokichi. Both break down and profess their Christianity. Then comes Kichijiro. He does what he is told and is set free. The other two will have to face the water punishment.

"Blood is flowing again"

Several days later, a little after noon, Ichizo and Mokichi are marched through the village to the beach while Rodrigues and Garrpe watch from their hut. The priests are told later what happens next.

At the water's edge, the two men are tied to wooden crosses. When the tide comes in, the cold waves begin to cover their feet and then the lower half of their bodies and finally up to their chins. A woman named Omatsu gets permission to take a boat out to the men to offer them food. To Mokichi, she whispers, "You will both go to Paradise."

Later, in the dark of night when no one can see the crosses anymore, the people on the shore hear Mokichi's voice singing a hymn: "We're on our way, we're on our way, we're on our way to the temple of Paradise."

After a day and a half, the two men are dead.

Rodrigues, trained as he has been in the idea of a "glorious martyrdom," is shocked when he is told how Mokichi and Ichizo came to die. For him, these deaths aren't "glorious" in any way. "What a miserable and painful business it was!"

It is only weeks later that Rodrigues himself witnesses a martyrdom. By this time, he is in prison, and from his cell he is watching as a panel of samurai attempts to convince five Christians — four men and the woman named Monica — to trample on a *fumi-e*, arguing that it is only a formality and "won't hurt your convictions."

The five refuse.

The samurai get up and adjourn to a nearby hut. The five Christians and their guards begin to talk with each other and joke. Then, one of the samurai comes out and tells the guards to send four of the Christians back to their cells but keep Chokichi, a one-eyed man also called Juan, out in the courtyard.

The afternoon is quiet, and Chokichi and the guard continue an amiable conversation.

Then, in a flash, a samurai runs out of the hut and, with a single swish of his sword, cuts off Chokichi's head. Monica screams and then struggles to begin a hymn.

A week later, Rodrigues witnesses Monica's martyrdom. She is one of the three Christians who are wrapped up tightly in straw mats "like basket worms" and pushed into the sea as a praying Garrpe swims out to them and dies as well.

Resolute, resigned, believing (despite the formality of their apostasy at the *fumi-e*), Monica and the other Christians die.

"Look!" the interpreter tells Rodrigues, "Blood is flowing again. The blood of those ignorant people is flowing again."

QUESTIONS FOR REFLECTION OR DISCUSSION

Why do you think the Japanese Christians are so willing to undergo torture and death for their faith? Do you understand their motivation? Why or why not?

Before his own apostasy, Ferreira calls the martyrs "heroes of Christ." How does their heroism compare with the decision of several priests, including Ferreira and Rodrigues, to ritually show their rejection of their Christian beliefs by placing their foot on wooden image of Jesus, a fumi-e? What constitutes heroism in faith today? Explain your answer.

What does it mean to you that, in the absence of priests, the secret community of Christians in Tomogi continued to express and pass along their faith through baptism, religious instruction, and prayer meetings? Has your faith ever been attacked or threatened? How did you react? Share the story if you can.

Are Ichizo and Mokichi wrong to be willing to "trample" an image of Jesus but not to say that Mary was a harlot? Give examples from your own life where you draw a line you cannot cross.

Why do you think that as Ichizo and Mokichi are tied to the crosses in the rising water along the shore Mokichi sings, "We're on our way...to the temple of Paradise"? What is your own vision of heaven, and how do you think people get there?

How would you describe the faith of the Japanese Christians? In what ways is it similar or different from your own?

CHAPTER THREE
THE FAITH OF INOUE,
GOVERNOR OF CHIKUGO

After several decades of persecution, it became clear that the efforts of Japanese officials to martyr thousands of Christians in public ceremonies had become counter-productive.

Indeed, the resolute willingness of missionaries and lay people alike to undergo horrible torments and then death rather than abjure their beliefs was fueling the spread of the now underground religion. In addition, the Christians were becoming more adept at hiding their faith and at pretending to be devout Buddhists.

But then onto the scene comes Inoue, the newly named Governor of Chikugo, a man "cunning as a serpent" and "a terror to the Christians." And a man filled with insidious new strategies for rooting out the European-based faith.

One strategy is the technique that his officials use in the trial of the Christians from Tomogi.

As they have been instructed by Father Sebastian Rodrigues, Mokichi and Ichizo go through the ritual of trampling the *fumi-e*, placing their foot on an image of the Virgin Mary and the Christ Child. However, the officials say this isn't enough. Inoue, who knows the devotion that many Japanese Christians have to the mother of Jesus, has told them to give the men a second demand — to spit on a crucifix and to say that the Blessed Virgin was a harlot. Neither man can do it, and they suffer martyrdom as a result.

Even more treacherous is the Inoue strategy that will bring Rodrigues to his crisis of faith.

Instead of battering the missionaries with terrible cruelty and, in the process, demonstrating the strength of their beliefs, Inoue spares them — spares them so that they can watch and hear as the members of their flocks undergo great tortures.

Instead of imposing physical anguish on a priest, he inflicts mental agonies. He turns the tables on them. He offers to relieve the suffering of the "small fry" if the priest will apostatize, if he will ritually put his foot upon an image of Jesus.

The message from Inoue is simple: By refusing to trample on the *fumi-e*, the priest himself is the one who is putting the Christians through these great tribulations. The priest himself is the torturer. In this way, the magistrate is able to apply enough guilt, pressure, and doubt that at least four missionary priests, including Rodrigues' highly respected teacher Father Christovao Ferreira, abandon their Christian faith. They publicly turn their backs on Christianity.

Inoue's past experience is the secret to his success — the fact that, thirty years earlier, he had studied with the missionaries and had been baptized as a Christian. Now, like a reverse St. Paul, he has turned his back on Christianity and is leading the persecution against the faith.

"In front of you"

The first time that an imprisoned Rodrigues is confronted by Inoue, he doesn't realize that the older chubby-faced samurai questioning him is the much-feared magistrate.

Instead, the Jesuit sees a man with big ears, a kindly smile, a gentle manner of speaking, and a child's curiosity, offering words of consolation. He even calls Rodrigues "Father" and engages him in an intellectual discussion.

"Father, we are not disputing about the right and wrong of your doctrine," the Governor says. "In Spain and Portugal and such countries it may be true. The reason we have outlawed Christianity in Japan is that, after deep and earnest consideration, we find its teaching to be of no value for Japan of today."

Rodrigues replies that truth is universal and goes on to debate learned points with the group of samurai while other Christians in the prison look on. As he does, the priest watches the old man nod at several points as if to say he is on the Jesuit's side. And Rodrigues begins to feel like a hero. It is in this frame of mind that he brags to the samurai that whatever answers he gives to their questions, he is going to be punished. It is his mark of honor, his badge of righteousness.

No, the old man says. He won't be harmed without reason.

Oh, yes, he will, Rodrigues responds. Why, if the old man were Inoue, he would strike the Jesuit down in an instant!

That statement evokes a loud laugh from the officials, and the priest, bewildered, asks what's so funny. "Father," says the interpreter, pointing at the old man, "this is Inoue, the Governor of Chikugo. He is here in front of you."

Rodrigues is agog. He can't believe that "this understanding, seemingly good, meek man" is the terrifying, Satan-like figure he has feared for so long.

A true believer

The magistrate and the priest meet two more times in *Silence*, once before Rodrigues' apostasy and once after. In both cases, Inoue is still grinning, even laughing, but the Jesuit realizes that despite the Governor's seeming merriment his brown eyes never smile. He is deadly serious.

At both meetings, Inoue tells Rodrigues that Christianity is so foreign to the Japanese culture and way of life that it can't take root. Unlike others who are taking part in the persecution, the magistrate tells the priest, he doesn't see Christianity as an evil religion — just totally wrong for Japan.

When it comes to his homeland, Inoue is a true believer.

In their second meeting, the Governor takes a bantering approach with Rodrigues, telling him about Takanobu Matsuura, the lord of the Hirado region in the late sixteenth century, who had four concubines who were always bickering and seeking special favor with him. One day, he got fed up and threw them out of his castle.

Rodrigues replies somewhat prudishly (and shortsightedly) that Matsuura was wise since he shouldn't have been living with concubines.

Ah, the magistrate says, that's good. All of Japan is like Matsuura: "Spain, Portugal, Holland, England and such-like women keep whispering jealous tales of slander into the ear of the man called Japan." And it's only reasonable for that man Japan to act like the lord of Hirado and outlaw these various versions of Christianity.

Why doesn't the man called Japan, the priest says, just choose a wife? Choose the Christian church as his spouse?

But, the Governor asks, why a foreign wife? Why not a wife from his own country "who has sympathy with his way of thinking"? The situation, he tells Rodrigues, is like a man who is suffering from "the persistent love of an ugly woman." Or a man who is being asked to marry a woman who cannot bear children. Inoue gets up, and as he leaves he tells the priest to ponder those two images.

When they meet again, Rodrigues has already put his foot on the image of the face of Jesus and, in doing so, has taken up a public identity as a Christian apostate. In their short conversation, Inoue seems to go out of his way to avoid mentioning that apostasy. He even refers again to the priest as "Father." Yet, it is clear that Rodrigues now belongs to Inoue and will belong to him for the rest of his life.

The Governor gives the priest a Japanese name, Okada San'emon, which used to belong to a man who recently died. He tells Rodrigues that he will now go to Edo to live in a house there and will take San'emon's wife as his own.

Christianity never had a chance in Japan, the magistrate says. It could never put down roots in any permanent way. It was defeated by "the swamp of Japan." Japanese people look to the Buddhist idea of mercy "out of hopeless weakness," he tells the priest. The idea of mercy in Christianity, though, not only calls on the believer to rely on God but also to exhibit "a strength of heart."

Rodrigues' own inability to stand fast under the mental torture that Inoue's officials inflicted on him is proof, the magistrate suggests, that the swamp of Japan has twisted and changed the religion. True, there are still pockets of Christians in the country, but they are so cut off from the missionaries that the faith that remains is being warped into something strange, something no longer "like the Christian God at all."

Inoue sighs and tells Rodrigues: "Japan is that kind of country. It can't be helped."

QUESTIONS FOR REFLECTION OR DISCUSSION

Inoue had been baptized as a Christian, but then he became one of the greatest and cleverest persecutors of Christians. What do you think is behind his reversal? Have you ever switched sides on an issue or changed your opinion of someone or something? Describe what happened.

Is Inoue evil? From a Christian point of view? From a Japanese patriot's point of view? Explain your two answers.

Does Inoue's argument that Christianity has "no value" for Japan make any sense to you? Why or why not? How does his view compare to some who say that Islam or atheism has "no value" for the United States?

Why does Inoue say Christianity is "an ugly woman"? What do you think about the use of metaphor in the Church? Describe some good examples and some bad examples.

In their final meeting, Inoue seems to take great pains not to remind Rodrigues directly of his apostasy, but he gives the priest a Japanese name and tells him he will marry a Japanese woman. Do you think he is he being cruel to the priest here, or kindly? Why?

How would you describe Inoue's faith? In what ways is it similar or different from your own?

CHAPTER FOUR
THE FAITH OF
FATHER CHRISTOVAO FERREIRA

In the end, they are "two ugly twins."

Father Christovao Ferreira and Father Sebastian Rodrigues — or, to use their new Japanese names, Sowano Chuan and Okada San'emon, names that symbolize the slicing of their ties to their European roots and European-based religion as well as their imprisonment within a strange and claustrophobic culture.

They despise each other. They hate each other. They pity each other. Yet, Endo writes, even the little neighborhood children know that they are inextricably linked. Ferreira, they call "Apostate Peter," and Rodrigues, "Apostate Paul." To the Dutch merchants who bring in ships to trade with the Japanese, they are simply "the apostate priests."

For Rodrigues, it is deeply painful even to be in the same room with Ferreira, "unbearable for him to see his own ugly face in the mirror that [is] Ferreira."

In the beginning, though, Ferreira had been his hero. For Rodrigues and his friends, he had been a beloved teacher, a kindly model of the priestly life, a fellow Jesuit, a Christian exemplar, a source of inspiration, and a courageous missionary who had spent decades in Japan to serve the Christian community despite the ever-present dangers of a brutal persecution. As an underground priest, Ferreira, a man of strength and vitality, had courted "a glorious martyrdom" for the faith.

His former students are shocked by reports that, after suffering the excruciating torture of the pit, their beloved teacher had betrayed his Christian beliefs and "groveled like a dog." They cajole their superiors to send them east to search for the truth. And, eventually, under cover of night, two of them — Rodrigues and Father Francis Garrpe — slip into Japan and begin serving a small, secret group of Christians near Nagasaki.

Rodrigues locates two old men who know something about Ferreira. They tell him that before the worst of the persecutions the priest had set up a house for abandoned infants and the sick, and Rodrigues imagines his mentor going about his day with his flock. He wonders "if he had mingled with these destitute Japanese Christians in the same way as he had with us students, putting his hand on their shoulders with the same friendly warmth." One of the old men tells him, "I have never met such a kind and gentle person in my life."

Another image of Ferreira, though, is forced upon the young Jesuit after he has been captured and is being cross-examined by an official he knows only as the interpreter, a man who once was in the seminary himself.

The interpreter tells the priest that he is sure Rodrigues will apostatize. For one thing, if he doesn't, five Christians will be tortured by being suspended over the pit. For another, he will soon be interrogated by Inoue, the Governor of Chikugo, who has already been able to persuade four priests to betray their faith — Porro, Pedro, Cassola, and Ferreira.

Ferreira?

He is alive, the interpreter says, and living in a mansion in Nagasaki. He has taken a Japanese name, and he has taken a Japanese wife.

It's ludicrous, Rodrigues says to himself, impossible. But, then, sobered at the thought that it might be true, he comes up against a bitter question: How will it be possible for him to have any chance to withstand Inoue and win "a glorious martyrdom" if even his hero couldn't?

"A beautiful exalted man"

The Ferreira whom Rodrigues finally encounters is drastically different from the one he knew back in Lisbon. Gone are his strength and pride and vitality. Gone too is his beard. He is now a thin, old man, dressed in a black kimono, disconsolate, with sunken cheeks, downcast eyes, and such an air of servility that, to his former student, he looks "just like a big animal which, with a rope around its neck, is trailed reluctantly along."

They meet in a dim temple, called Saishoji, and sit together face-to-face on the floor, as the interpreter and a bonze (Buddhist monk) look on while two or three chickens strut and peck nearby.

Rodrigues calls him "Father," and, with a quick, weak, servile smile, the emaciated Ferreira gives a glimpse of his deep shame. But only for a moment. Then the older man stares at Rodrigues with a challenge in his eyes.

What does Ferreira do all day?

The question from the younger priest causes Ferreira great pain. At the order of Inoue, he says, he is translating a book about astronomy. "I am of some use," he says. "I am of some use to the people of this country." And he says it two more times.

Rodrigues hears this as an attempt by the disgraced Jesuit to cling to his former dream of living a life of service "like a crazy woman who offers her breast to a baby."

Oh, but not just a book on astronomy, the interpreter injects. Ferreira, he crows, is also writing a book to refute and detail the errors of Christianity, a book that Inoue has read and praised. A mortified Ferreira looks off to the side and watches the chickens go about their mindless pecking. Rodrigues pictures his former teacher bent over a desk, betraying, with each line he writes, the faith to which he had devoted his life. "Worse than any torture!" he says and notices a tear in the eye of Ferreira.

Egged on by the interpreter, the older priest shows Rodrigues a brown scar behind his ear and explains that it's from a cut that was made just before he was tied up tightly and hung upside down over a pit filled with excrement. Blood from the cut slowly seeped down and fell from his face into the pit as, drop by drop, he was bleeding, by minute degrees, to death.

"Think it over," the interpreter says. After all, he argues, no religion should try to bring in new adherents. Buddhism? Christianity? — they're the same. All that matters is to "walk the path of truth."

The desolate Ferreira says to Rodrigues that, after working for twenty years as a missionary in Japan, he knows better than the newly ordained priest. And what he knows is that he was defeated because "our religion does not take root in this country."

Forlornly, robotically, he makes an argument that Rodrigues will later hear from Inoue as well — Japan is a swamp where anything that is planted rots, decays, and dies. True, Ferreira says, Christianity seemed to make great inroads initially. Under the surface, however, the Japanese way of life and way of thinking were subverting the message of the missionaries. "What the Japanese of that time believed in was not our God," he says. "It was their own gods." They twisted and distorted the faith like a butterfly caught in the web of a spider that becomes a skeleton of itself.

Rodrigues refuses to accept this. He has seen the martyrs, he has seen them die with a bright flame of faith.

No, says Ferreira. It is impossible for the Japanese to envision anything but this physical world. Those who died, he says, weren't dying for the Christian God but for some "beautiful exalted man."

"Not snoring"

Rodrigues' second encounter with Ferreira comes at the crucial moment of the young man's life.

"Now," the older Jesuit tells him, "you are going to perform the most painful act of love that has ever been performed." He says this a few feet away from the pit where, Endo writes, Rodrigues can hear the groans of three Christians as they suffer great torments for their faith.

Initially, however, in the dark of a long night, the youthful priest misunderstands the sounds he is hearing from his cell. It is, he thinks, some carefree soul, a guard probably, drunk on sake, who has fallen asleep and is now blissfully snoring. Then, at his doorway, are the interpreter and Ferreira. When Rodrigues complains about the snoring, Ferreira enlightens him.

"That's not snoring. That is the moaning of Christians hanging in the pit."

In the darkness, Rodrigues can't see Ferreira, but he can hear him clearly as he says in a sorrowful whisper that he was held in the same cell, and he too heard the groaning of those hanging over the pit.

Although Ferreira had carved the Latin words *Laudate Eum*," meaning "praise God," on the wall of the cell, he found, he says, as his own crucial night wore on, that he could no longer praise God. For three days, he himself had hung over the pit without giving in, but, then, he heard those voices of five victims and "God did nothing."

So he acted to relieve their pain, and now that is Rodrigues' task. By refusing to apostatize, the thin old man says, the young priest is making himself and his reputation and his salvation more important than those being tortured.

"If Christ were here...," the older man says, and then after a pause adds, "Certainly Christ would have apostatized to help men." For love, he says, Jesus would have done this.

And now the door of the cell is opened, and Ferreira takes the young man by his shoulders and guides him down a corridor to a spot where the interpreter has placed a large wooden plaque with the face of Christ crowned with thorns.

"Courage!" he says.

"Apostate Peter" and "Apostate Paul"

Ferreira and Rodrigues spend the rest of their lives as state prisoners under a comfortable but deeply constricting house arrest.

Both write books they are told to write. Both are brought in when strange, seemingly religious European objects turn up and are required to explain their significance.

They are "Apostate Peter" and "Apostate Paul."

They hate and scorn each other, but nonetheless they are "two ugly twins."

QUESTIONS FOR REFLECTION OR DISCUSSION

How difficult do you think it is for Ferreira to write the book in which he refutes Christianity? Why? If you had to try to refute your own religion, what is the major point you would make?

Ferreira argues that, by translating Western books into Japanese, he's being useful to the Japanese. Why do you think he emphasizes his usefulness so much? Do you ever do this? If you do, give an example of when and how it happens.

The interpreter says all religions are the same. Does Ferreira agree? Do you? Why or why not? Or maybe how and how not?

By calling Japan a swamp, is Ferreira asserting that the Japanese will never be able to find their way to God? Do you feel that certain peoples or countries are in this position? Why? Name them.

When he says, "Courage!" to Rodrigues before the younger man's apostasy, is Ferreira trying to help him or trick him? Why do you think so? Have you ever tried to support someone who had to do something difficult or even abhorrent? Describe your motives and actions.

How would you describe Ferreira's faith? In what ways is it similar or different from your own?

CHAPTER FIVE
THE FAITH OF KICHIJIRO

Father Sebastian Rodrigues despises the Japanese peasant Kichijiro for his weakness. He is disgusted by him for the "stench of his filth and sweat," his yellow eyes, and his "foul breath." He looks down on him as no better than a whipped dog. For the priest, the young Japanese is a coward who looks "just like a mouse ready to scamper off at the slightest thing" and a drunk who is "just like a pig that buried its face in its own vomit."

Yet, more than anyone else in *Silence*, Kichijiro shares Rodrigues' journey with him, accompanying the Portuguese Jesuit as he makes the long and painful trip through the dark night of his soul.

And he is there at the end, by then in his fifties, as an attendant of Rodrigues, serving the disgraced priest as he lives out the rest of his days under house arrest in his new Japanese incarnation as Okada San'emon.

In the course of Shusaku Endo's novel, Kichijiro apostatizes three times. Even as others — his family, his fellow Christians — stand fast for their faith and suffer great tortures and death, he in his fear and frailty is quick to step on an image of Jesus, to call Mary a whore, to spit on a crucifix. He even betrays Rodrigues to the authorities, out of greed, perhaps, or terror.

Yet, again and again, Kichijiro returns to the priest to seek forgiveness, to ask for the absolution of confession. "Father, what can I do, a weak person like me?"

"The cowardly weakling"

Kichijiro is the first Japanese that Rodrigues and Father Francis Garrpe meet. They have just arrived in Macao, and they go to a house to
find a man who, they have been told, wants to return to his homeland.

They find a fisherman in his late twenties who stumbles into the
room wearing rags and reeking of booze. Kichijiro is jittery and has
a crafty look in his eye. The two priests judge him to be a "cowardly
weakling," but they have no better candidate, so they ask him to come
to Japan with them as their guide.

Upon landing on the Japanese shore, Kichijiro does exactly what
they need. As Garrpe and Rodrigues cower in the dark, hidden on the
shore, Kichijiro makes contact with the local Japanese Christians and
brings them to the priests.

Only later do the Jesuits learn Kichijiro's story. Eight years earlier, he had been a Christian on the island of Fukazawa when he and
his family were brought in for questioning. His brothers and sisters
refused to trample on the *fumi-e*, but Kichijiro, with little prodding,
agreed to put his foot on the image of Jesus.

He was set free. His siblings were taken to prison, and later they
were burned at the stake. In the crowd that witnessed the martyrdom
was Kichijiro, who watched until he could watch no more.

Now, Kichijiro is part of the Christian community that Garrpe and
Rodrigues serve in the village of Tomogi. And his story repeats itself.

Samurai and guards sweep into the village and ransack it from top
to bottom, seeking evidence of Christian beliefs. Although they find
none, they take one hostage and, the next day, they demand three
more.

Kichijiro, as an outsider in the village, is brow-beaten into volun-
teering to be one of the hostages. "From sheer weakness he could no
longer refuse," Rodrigues writes to his superiors. Two of the lay leaders in the village, Mokichi and Ichizo, also agree to go. When they are

tested, they follow the instructions they received from Rodrigues to put their foot on the image of Jesus. But then the authorities demand that the Christians say the Blessed Virgin is a prostitute and also spit on a crucifix.

Mokichi and Ichizo are unable to carry out this additional sacrilege and are later martyred, tied to crosses in the rising and falling tide along the shore. Kichijiro spits and blasphemes, and he goes free.

And, then, it happens a third time.

"A weak person like me"

Rodrigues is hiding in the hills when he comes across Kichijiro again. He fears that the young man will betray him, but he feels lost and alone. He is desperately hungry, and the Japanese peasant gives him dried fish. The meal, though, leaves the priest parched the next day, and Kichijiro goes off and brings back a pitcher of water for him.

He also brings back guards who arrest the Jesuit and give the betrayer tiny silver coins. "Father, forgive me!" a kneeling, mournful Kichijiro says. "I am weak." He has, Rodrigues thinks, "fearful eyes like a spider."

Yet, weak as his is, Kichijiro follows Rodrigues from a distance as the priest is taken to prison.

From a boat, the priest sees the figure of what looks like a beggar running along the shore, shouting. Even as he runs, Kichijiro trips in the sand, but gets himself up and continues after the boat, and trips again, and rises again, and runs again after the Jesuit, all the time shouting in a voice that sounds like hissing and weeping. Finally, he stops and, as the boat gets farther and farther away, stands there, motionless and desolate, watching Rodrigues get smaller and smaller.

Soon enough, though, Rodrigues, riding on a horse amid a pack of guards, still on his way to prison, sees Kichijiro again, this time walking along next to the procession. When he realizes that the priest has spotted him, Kichijiro hides behind a tree. The samurai stop for a meal, and Rodrigues is tied to a tree and offered no food. But out of a pack of beggars comes a man who gives the priest some rice in a broken dish. It is Kichijiro. He returns to the group of beggars and squats with them occasionally "raising his eyes like a whipped dog."

At last the procession reaches the prison, and Rodrigues is put in his cell. Soon enough, there is a disturbance at the gate of the compound. In the rain, the guards are yelling at a man in a cape who is pleading for something. They wave a stick at him, and he scurries away "like a wild dog." But quickly he's back again, quiet this time, and he stands there in the downpour as the hours tick away.

It is Kichijiro. Despite a look of fear that crosses his face when he realizes that Rodrigues is looking at him, he calls out to the priest. He acknowledges that, unlike Mokichi and Ichizo, he betrayed the faith. "I can't be strong like them," he says.

At this, the guards come out of their hut and again chase Kichijiro away. Yet, as he leaves, he shouts that he hated to apostatize, that his feet ached with pain afterwards. "God asks me to imitate the strong, even though he made me weak. Isn't this unreasonable?" Again and again, Kichijiro tries to return and is driven away by the guards. "Father, what can I do, a weak person like me?"

Finally, he yells to the guards that he is a Christian and belongs in the prison, and so they drag him into a cell with other believers.

When Rodrigues gets a chance to visit that cell, he finds that the prisoners won't have anything to do with Kichijiro, fearing that he is a spy for the authorities. Kichijiro pleads with the priest to hear his confession and says, "I am an apostate; but if I had died ten years ago I might have gone to paradise as a good Christian, not despised as an apostate. Merely because I live in a time of persecution.... I am sorry."

Rodrigues is nauseated by the odor of the thin, ragged man, "this dirtiest of men," and holds him in such contempt that he says to himself that Kichijiro is so weak he can't even be called evil. Nonetheless, the priest gives him absolution and tells him to go in peace.

And, within a few hours, Kichijiro apostatizes his third time.

Five of the Christians are lined up in an open area and ordered to trample the *fumi-e*. They refuse. Four are sent back to their cell, but one, the one-eyed man named Chokichi, is left squatting in the sun, talking affably with his guard. Suddenly, a samurai races out of a nearby hut, swinging his long sword and slicing Chokichi's head from his body. It is the first martyrdom of a Japanese Christian that Rodrigues witnesses.

Then, into one of the cells run the guards, and out they bring Kichijiro, trembling and bowing repeatedly. At their insistence, he puts his foot onto the image of Jesus. "Get out!" one yells, and Kichijiro leaves, stumbling and hurrying away. But he is not gone from Rodrigues' life.

Some days later, the priest is put on a horse amid a group of guards for a journey to the new prison where he will face the reality of the pit. Dozens of Japanese along the road stare at him with astonishment and enmity, and one throws a hunk of horse manure at him. Buddhist monks threaten him with sticks. Amid all this hostility, he sees Kichijiro, wearing rags, looking like a dog, cowering — the only person the priest knows.

At the new prison, in the dark of the night when Rodrigues will be tested to the utmost, a familiar scene repeats itself.

Kichijiro is wanting to get in, telling the guards that he is a Christian and needs to see the priest. The guards think he is crazy. "Father, forgive me!" he shouts in the darkness. He is hit by the jailer, but shouts it again. Bitterly, the priest silently recites the words of absolution.

"I was born weak," Kichijiro shouts. "One who is weak of heart cannot die a martyr.... Ah, why was I born into the world at all?"

An attendant to Rodrigues

After Rodrigues apostatizes and is given a Japanese name and a Japanese wife and is set up in a home where he lives under house arrest, Kichijiro follows him and becomes one of his attendants.

He is still getting in trouble. At the age of fifty-four, Kichijiro is sent to jail because he has been found with a medal with Sts. Peter and Paul on one side and the Jesuit missionary Francis Xavier and an angel on the other. He tells his interrogator that it had been dropped three years earlier by a visitor and he had picked it up.

His jailers think he may have gotten it from Rodrigues, now called Okada San'emon, but Kichijiro says that's impossible since guards are always with the priest. The priest is questioned and denies that he has ever tried to convert Kichijiro.

QUESTIONS FOR REFLECTION OR DISCUSSION

Why do you think Kichijiro apostatizes and then tries to rejoin the Christian community? Have you ever been ambivalent about your religious and spiritual beliefs? Describe when and why, if you can.

How does Kichijiro's weakness contrast with the willingness of so many of his fellow Japanese Christians to undergo torture and death for their faith? Is he just more realistic than they are, or is he merely a coward? Do you ever have to make decisions like this? Do you ever rationalize? Describe.

How does Kichijiro's apostasy compare to the apostasy of Rodrigues? Are there levels of betrayal? What are they?

Do you think Kichijiro as loathsome as Rodrigues sees him? Why or why not?

Kichijiro says over and over that he is a weak person, not strong enough to be a martyr. Is this a cop-out? Have you ever felt weak or powerless? Tell the story, if you can.

How would you describe the faith of Kichijiro? In what ways is it similar or different from your own?

PART TWO
THE FAITH OF FATHER SEBASTIAN RODRIGUES

In its jarring polyphony and its silences,
the book of Job speaks to and for the broken.
In its protagonist's persistence,
it speaks of hope even in the depths of despair.

"THE BOOK OF 'JOB': A BIOGRAPHY,"
MARK LARRIMORE

CHAPTER SIX
RODRIGUES AS A EUROPEAN

Father Sebastian Rodrigues is being held by guards in a small hut, and into the hut steps a Japanese man who surprises the priest by greeting him in Portuguese. "The pronunciation was strange and halting, but it was certainly Portuguese."

The samurai introduces himself as an interpreter but provides no name. He tells Rodrigues that he learned Portuguese in the seminary. He is quick, though, to explain that he was never a believer in Christianity. As the son of a court samurai, he saw that his only route to success in life was through learning. Now he uses his knowledge of Portuguese and Christianity in the service of the authorities, such as Inoue.

As the interpreter talks on, Rodrigues dismisses the rush of words as prattling. He keeps a stone face, refusing to talk.

This angers the interpreter, and the man tells Rodrigues that the seminary priests weren't so silent. Indeed, they were quick to ridicule their Japanese students. One, in particular, Father Cabral "had nothing but contempt for everything Japanese. He despised our houses; he despised our language; he despised our food and our customs...." Cabral's anti-Japanese bias was so strong that he wouldn't permit the ordination of Japanese men who had graduated from the seminary.

The priest remains silent. He has heard stories about Cabral from other Jesuits and knows that Cabral's enmity drove some Japanese lay people and priests away from the Christian faith.

"I'm not like Cabral," he says finally.

"Really?" the interpreter replies. "I'm not so sure."

"Ignorant beasts"

When arguing for permission to go to Japan, Rodrigues and his two friends asserted that their goal wasn't only to determine the fate of Father Christovao Ferreira, their old teacher. In addition, they wanted to serve the Japanese people — "to give them courage and to ensure that the tiny flame of faith does not die out."

But, after traveling more than a year from Europe to China and finally to Japan, Rodrigues is deeply disoriented by the life he finds in his new land.

Although he has been sent to minister to the Japanese Christians, the Jesuit makes little human contact with them as people. Instead, it is as if there is a great wall or a deep chasm that separates the priest from his flock. The food, the clothing, the smells, the culture — all of these feel oppressive to Rodrigues.

"I am at the end of the earth," he writes in one of his letters to Portugal. In another, he tells his superiors of returning from a visit to the Christian community on a nearby island and how this filled him with joy and happiness. "I am of some use to the people of this country at the ends of the earth, I reflected — a people and a country which you can never understand."

So alien is this land, so unsettling is its strangeness, that Rodrigues takes great comfort when a Japanese Christian first greets him with the word "Padre" because it is "spoken in our own beloved Portuguese tongue...something we never dreamt of hearing in this place."

Later, though, he has a different reaction when he hears his Japanese flock praying. He can't stop himself from "laughing when I hear the mumbling Portuguese and Latin words in the mouths of these ignorant peasants." There is much about Japanese customs that irritates and aggravates Rodrigues. Their names are odd and difficult to remember. They all look alike, and it makes the priest feel embarrassed when, as he frequently does, he calls one by another's name. They even have a "queer way of sitting — completely different from ours." They kneel on the ground and then sit back on their heels. Squatting like this, he writes, is restful for them but very painful for Rodrigues.

To him, the Japanese peasants look like puppets, their faces expressionless whether confronting the cruelties of a hard life or standing before anti-Christian officials. His reading of the situation is that, because they have had to live with so much secrecy to avoid persecution, their faces have become masks that don't register joy or sorrow. "The wisdom of peasants shows itself in their ability to pretend that they are fools," he writes in one letter.

These blank faces are what he fixates on, not on something more positive, such as the joy that two of the Christian men show when they are given crucifixes by the priests.

The same is true when Rodrigues watches the Japanese cultivate their small plots of wheat and potatoes. He recognizes how hard the work is and how dogged they are to scratch a living from the soil. Yet what strikes him more is the cruelty of the life they lead, and he equates them with beasts of burden. Like cattle and horses, he writes in a letter back to Portugal, they live, and like cattle and horses, they die.

During the first baptism that the two priests conduct in Japan, Rodrigues devotes little thought to the sacramental meaning of the rite. Instead, as Father Francis Garrpe recites the prayers next to him, Rodrigues focuses on the small broken peasant's cup that they must use for the holy water. The ritual, he writes, is touching and thrilling. Still, he dwells on what he sees as the brutish nature of the people.

The tiny baby wrinkles "its face" and cries loudly, he writes, not even noticing if the infant is a boy or a girl. He does notice, though, that "this was already a peasant face." The baby will grow into adulthood "in this cramped and desolate land," and echoing what he wrote earlier Rodrigues sees no other possible future but that this child will live and die "like a beast."

As Endo unfolds the story of *Silence*, he has Rodrigues use the same words over and over again to describe the peasants — as cattle, as "ignorant beasts." Yet, it's not just the peasants.

When the priest is being interrogated by a smiling pudgy samurai, he thinks of the man as "simple as a child" and sees him as a monkey. In fact, he uses that term twice, including when he thinks he is getting the upper hand in their give-and-take: "He even began to feel a secret joy in teasing this old fellow who looked like a monkey."

"The stench of fish"

It doesn't occur to Rodrigues that these Japanese, whether the Christians or the chubby samurai, are people like he is. He thinks of them as if they were beings on another planet, a planet called Japan.

There is nothing in his letters back to Europe or in his thoughts after his capture that indicates any empathy toward them. He seems incapable of understanding that they tell jokes and sing songs and make love and feel happiness at times and sadness at others — that they experience the full range of emotions that any European, that any human, does.

Instead, for him, the Japanese are like little children and like beasts, mindless and emotionless as they go through life, like insects crawling up the wall.

Rodrigues signals this early in *Silence* in his third letter back home when he writes that, without Christianity, the lives of the Japanese are nothing. Belief in Jesus, he asserts, has spread as far as it has, "like water flowing into dry earth," because "it has given to this group of people a human warmth they never previously knew." The waves of missionaries have "treated them like human beings...the human kindness and charity of the fathers...touched their hearts." In other words, the priest's view is that until the Europeans arrived in Japan the people knew nothing about kindness and charity, knew nothing about what it was like to live as a human being.

This is an example of cultural paternalism at its worst. From the perspective of Rodrigues, Europeans know what's right and lesser people need to listen to their betters to know how they should act.

The priest is also perturbed when the Japanese identify too closely with the European culture. On his way to prison, a bedraggled Rodrigues is thrown in with a handful of peasant Christians whom he describes as "ignorant beasts." A woman asks the priest if he would like something to eat, and from her bosom she takes out a couple cucumbers. One, she eats. The other, she gives to Rodrigues.

He forgets her kindness, however, when he asks her name. "Monica," she says, as though her Christian name was "the only ornament she possessed in the whole world." This angers Rodrigues; it seems so improper. What priest, he wonders, gave the name of St. Augustine's mother "to this woman whose body was reeking with the stench of fish?"

The priest has the same reaction to the way the peasants think about their faith and about eternal life with God in heaven.

When two of the Christian leaders from Tomogi are tied to crosses as the waves of the sea rise up their bodies, one has enough strength to sing: "We're on our way, we're on our way, we're on our way to the temple of Paradise."

Later, Monica talks about the faith that was behind the song. "Brother Ishida," she says, "used to say that when we go to Heaven we will find there everlasting peace and happiness. There we will not have to pay taxes every year, nor worry about hunger and illness. There will be no hard labor there."

In response, Rodrigues says some soothing words, but in his heart he thinks it is a childish idea, not worthy of the theological intricacies that he has learned. In his heart, he wants to shout, "Heaven is not the sort of place you think it is!"

QUESTIONS FOR REFLECTION OR DISCUSSION

Why do you think Father Cabral despises the Japanese? Have you ever been prejudiced or the victim of prejudice? What happened? What was the end result?

What does it mean to Rodrigues to find himself "at the end of the earth"? Have you ever felt that way? Describe what happened.

Rodrigues experiences much about life in Japan as annoying, such as the difficulty he has in telling people apart, the way the people squat, how odd their names sound. For an outsider, are there other responses to such cultural differences? Name some of them.

Rodrigues says the wisdom of the peasants is to be able to look like fools. Do you think he meant that as a compliment? Why or why not? Have you ever tried to hide your emotions or blend into a crowd? What happened?

Why do you think Rodrigues is so oppressed by the peasant way of life? Why does he react to the peasant baby at the baptism the way he does? Rodrigues says the peasants only found kindness and charity when the priests arrived. What do you think he meant by that? Was it merely self-serving, or do priests and religious have something special to offer? If so, what is it?

Why do you think Rodrigues is upset that Monica has the name of St. Augustine's mother? Why is he upset at the way Monica pictures heaven? Do you ever feel negatively about other's people's piety? Explain.

How would you describe Rodrigues' faith? In what ways is it similar or different from your own?

CHAPTER SEVEN
RODRIGUES AND
THE GLORIOUS MARTYRDOM

In the bright midday sun, the heat in the courtyard is oppressive and the humidity is thick. A cicada in a nearby tree chirps its rapid, machine-like mating call.

Father Sebastian Rodrigues, sweating and awkward in his ill-fitting Japanese clothing, stands before a panel of five samurai, a powerless prisoner. But he's happy. For the first time since coming to Japan, he feels truly comfortable. With Christian prisoners in their cells around the courtyard listening intently, he has been debating with the samurai about culture, truth, and religious faith.

It is a controversy, an intellectual disputation in which cleverness and mental agility are important skills. A battle of minds and a battle of wills. This is what he has been trained for; this is what he spent years in the seminary preparing for — to defend the faith against the heathen with all the arguments of the great Christian thinkers at his fingertips: St. Thomas Aquinas, St. Augustine, St. Anselm, and all the others.

And he's winning!

"Even as he spoke," writes Shusaku Endo, "he felt an onrush of emotion. The more conscious he became of being watched by the Christians from behind, the more he went on making himself a hero." This is the heroic priesthood to which Rodrigues has long aspired. The priest as the center of all attention. The priest as the bearer of all wisdom, the distributor of truth, the opener of eyes. God's voice to the multitudes.

It isn't just the listening Christians who give Rodrigues the flood of triumph that fills his body. Even more, it's the one samurai in the chair on the extreme right, a kindly looking, big-eared old man "with the curiosity of a child." Speaking gently, this samurai calls Rodrigues "Father" and says he is moved by the strength of the priest's resolution to brave such a long journey and so many hardships to travel from Europe to Japan. The old man smiles, seemingly sympathetic, as the interpreter for the panel tells the Jesuit that his judges aren't here to argue about the validity of Christianity. It is a faith that may be worthwhile in Europe, but here in Japan it has no value.

The debate is on.

Truth is universal, says Rodrigues, lecturing the five samurai, casting a friendly smile in the direction of the older one. Why else would the missionaries travel so far and put up with so much? They come to Japan to bring a great gift. After all, how could something be "true" if it weren't true everywhere? The old samurai is nodding his head. He seems to be in complete agreement.

One of the others, through the interpreter, jousts with the priest, arguing that a tree may thrive in one type of soil but not in another. When the tree of Christianity is planted in Japan, he says, "the leaves wither and no bud appears." Ah, but the buds did appear and the leaves were thick and green, Rodrigues counters. When the Japanese authorities permitted their people to join the Church, Christianity thrived. Hundreds of thousands joined! Leaves won't grow and flowers won't blossom without fertilizer.

Rodrigues feels that he is scoring points as the game of the debate goes forward. Four of the samurai and the interpreter look tense and tight, but not the old man. He continues to nod and seems to be entirely on the priest's side. So much so that, for Rodrigues, "a pleasant emotion rose slowly within his breast."

It is then that the Jesuit plays his trump card. He insists he is not stupid. He knows that nothing he says will change their minds. Even so, he asserts that he will remain stalwart in his faith and firm in his resolve. He is ready for his glorious martyrdom. "No matter what I say, I will be punished."

At that, the mood of the examination changes. The old man starts shaking his head, as if to "a naughty child," and tells Rodrigues that he is mistaken, that no priest is punished without reason.

Of course, he will be punished, Rodrigues says. "If you were Inoue you would punish me instantly."

With that, Rodrigues loses. The samurai all laugh.

The old man, he learns to his chagrin, is Inoue. The man who, to the priest, looks as "naïve as a child," a man who seems so quiet and humane — this is the man he has feared and loathed from afar.

Inoue stands up and leads the samurai away. Rodrigues has been made to look a fool, but he refuses to see himself that way. Instead, "a violent emotion" rises in his chest and his eyes fill with tears and he feels that he has achieved something great. Behind him, the Christian prisoners sing: "We're on our way, we're on our way, we're on our way to the temple of Paradise."

Even after he is marched back to his cell, Rodrigues remains happy.

He has defended Christianity and, despite his laughable mistake, hasn't harmed the faith of his flock. He has not been dishonorable. He has not been a coward.

He has been a hero.

A "hero of Christ"

This scene, from midway through Endo's *Silence*, provides a window into Rodrigues' soul and into his concept of his priesthood.

As a European, he is weighed down by the all-perplexing alienness of everything in Japan, from the food to the people to the clothing to the cicadas. His spirit is deeply agitated. Not least of all because this isn't the way it should be. It isn't the way it was. The way it used to be. Not at all.

For forty years, scores of Christian missionaries — led first by the famed Jesuit St. Francis Xavier (canonized while Rodrigues was in the seminary) — had come to Japan to be greeted with open arms. Rodrigues recalled those days in one of his letters back to Portugal: "When they came to Japan, fortune smiled gaily upon their every venture. Everywhere was safe for them.... The feudal lords vied with one another to give them protection — not from any love of their faith but out of a desire for trade."

Indeed, circumstances so blessed the missionaries that at one point they weighed, with appropriate seriousness, the question of whether their cassocks should remain cotton or be made of silk.

The Japanese people brought the fathers gifts of fish and rice and rushed to be baptized. The priests had all the bread and wine they needed for the Holy Sacrifice of the Mass. There were dozens of churches — eleven in Nagasaki alone — filled with the music of harp and organ. And, in two seminaries, Japanese boys chanted Latin.

A great cathedral was erected by the Jesuits on a hill overlooking Nagasaki, and also a huge crucifix that could be sighted by faraway ships approaching the harbor. On Easter Sunday, Japanese Christians, carrying candles and singing hymns, would walk in procession to the top of the hill. The faith was "fragrant like the fresh flowers of the morning."

Then, the persecutions began. On a daily basis, scores of missionaries and Japanese Christians were publicly tortured with great cruelty and put to death with great pain and horror. Yet the faith continued to thrive underground. Priests continued to smuggle themselves into Japan to serve the faithful and, ultimately, to give their lives as martyrs for the glory of God.

When Father Christovao Ferreira wrote to his superiors about the torments that five priests and two women underwent for the faith, he rejoiced at how their bravery and steadfastness had been a beacon of strength to other believers. Indeed, their resolute acceptance of suffering in the name of Jesus had touched the hearts of many Japanese and led them to Christianity. The priests had shown their persecutors that "all the springs in Unzen would run dry before men of such power could be persuaded to change their minds." They were, Ferreira wrote, "heroes of Christ."

A "hero of Christ" is what Rodrigues wants to be.

He longs for "a glorious martyrdom." In fact, it has been his dream from his youth to end his life with such a triumph: "I had long read about martyrdom in the lives of the saints — how the souls of the martyrs had gone home to Heaven, how they had been filled with glory in Paradise, how the angels had blown trumpets. This was the splendid martyrdom I had often seen in my dreams."

Rodrigues wants to be a hero, a gloriously tragic hero. He wants to be a saint. After all, as he says, even the last priest remaining in Japan will have "the same significance as a single candle burning in the catacombs." Rodrigues is in Japan, Endo writes, "to lay down his life for other men."

But as he looks at his life in this foreign land, the imprisoned Rodrigues is discontented and resentful. He feels "an inexpressible dissatisfaction — a kind of disillusionment that he was not privileged to be a tragic hero like so many martyrs and like Christ himself." Instead, other Christians are "laying down their lives one by one for him."

And their martyrdoms are far from glorious. When Mokichi and Ichizo are lashed to crosses in the rising and receding tide, it takes days for them to slowly succumb to their sufferings. Rodrigues writes back to Europe about the atrocity of their deaths and describes how the martyrdom was nothing like what he had expected, what he had dreamed of. Their martyrdom "was no such glorious thing. What a miserable and painful business it was!"

The priest's reaction is the same to the sudden, brutal beheading of Chokichi, the one-eyed man also called Juan. One moment, the Japanese is talking pleasantly with a guard in the prison courtyard and, the next, "black blood is flowing" from his severed neck, staining the sand "like the sash of a garment."

Even as the body is dragged away, the cicada continues its monotonous, mindless clicking, and a shaken Rodrigues is bewildered: "Just as before, a fly kept buzzing around the priest's face. In the world outside there was no change. A man had died, but there was no change." And no trumpeting angels. "A man had died. Yet the outside world went on as if nothing had happened. Could anything be more crazy? Was this martyrdom?"

Rodrigues wonders if, on the day of his own death, the world will remain as indifferent as it is now to the death of the one-eyed man. Will the cicadas keep chirping? Will the flies keep buzzing?

The life of a priest and a triumphant martyrdom has been Rodrigues' "glorious dream." But the longer he is in Japan, the more he experiences the warping and twisting of that vision. Indeed, the priest is told more than once by the interpreter that his yearning for martyrdom and refusal to apostatize are resulting in the torments and executions of the Christians he is in Japan to serve.

"It is," the interpreter taunts him, "the Japanese who have to die for your selfish dreams."

QUESTIONS FOR REFLECTION OR DISCUSSION

Rodrigues hopes to be a hero and a saint. Is this a good goal to have? Can it be subverted? Explain your answers. Why is Rodrigues hopeful for a "glorious martyrdom"? Are you? Why or why not?

Why do you think Inoue nods and smiles as Rodrigues debates the other samurai? Have you ever found yourself in this position? Tell the story. When he gets back to his cell, the priest tells himself that, despite his gaffe over Inoue's identity, he did well in the debate. Do you think he was right? Have you ever thought you did better in a situation than you did? How did you find out otherwise? How did it make you feel?

Rodrigues argues that something that is "true" one place has to be true everywhere. Is that correct? What do you mean by "has"?

Why do the martyrdoms of the Japanese lay people seem so "miserable" to Rodrigues? How do they seem to you? How is the life of a Christian different before and after the beginning of a persecution? Is there a lesson in that difference for those of us living in the modern world?

Rodrigues is shocked that the cicada kept chirping and the world went along as usual after the sudden beheading of the one-eyed man. Why? The interpreter tells him that his desire to bring Christianity to Japan is a "selfish dream." Why do you think he says that? Do you agree? Why or why not?

How would you describe Rodrigues' faith as he presents it to his Japanese inquisitors? In what ways would you defend your faith similarly or differently from Rodrigues?

CHAPTER EIGHT
RODRIGUES AND PRIESTLY DUTY

Since arriving in Japan, Father Sebastian Rodrigues has lived an Alice-in-Wonderland, upside-down existence. All the verities of his life seem to have been warped and distorted to such an extent that he has a hard time recognizing them. It is as if he is looking in the crazy reflection of a carnival mirror.

And nothing seems crazier than the fact that, after months in Japan, he is finally able to live fully his life as a priest in the one place he'd never expected to — prison.

While earlier missionaries have undergone great agonies, even to the point of being roasted alive, even to the point of being crucified for their faith, Rodrigues finds that in prison he is permitted for the first time to carry out his priestly duties in public and with relative ease. Indeed, he finds that his life as a captive is filled with "tranquility and peace."

The guards give him paper and string from which he fashions a rosary, and, throughout the day, he tolls his paper beads "biting at the sacred words." He asks permission to visit the Christian prisoners as they work in nearby fields, and it is granted. "Oh, it's the father," says Monica, the woman who on their march to the prison had shared with him a cucumber she had hidden in her bosom. With her is the one-eyed Chokichi.

From then on, Rodrigues goes daily from his cell to the one in which the handful of Christians are being held. It isn't so much that the guards are lax, although they are somewhat easy-going. It is, he knows, because the Christian prisoners are less likely to cause trouble if they can look forward to visits by the priest.

The Jesuit leads his tiny flock in reciting the Our Father, the Hail Mary, and the Creed. Although he can't say Mass since he has no bread and wine, he nonetheless preaches from the Psalms: "Put not your trust in princes; in the children of men, in whom there is no salvation. His spirit shall go forth, and he shall return into his earth; in that day all their thoughts shall perish. Blessed is he who hath the God of Jacob for his helper, whose hope is in the Lord his God, who made heaven and earth, the sea, and all things that are in them.... Blessed are the dead who die in the Lord."

As he speaks, the Christian prisoners — and the guards, as well — lean in with rapt attention. He tells them that their suffering will not grow worse, that God will not forsake them, will not remain silent.

When the prisoners are marched out to work, Rodrigues reaches through the opening in his door through which food is passed and blesses each on the forehead with the Sign of the Cross. In the evenings, he hears confessions by standing at the door of their cell and putting his ear to the opening there. Each person comes in turn and whispers his or her sins and is absolved. Back in his cell, the priest hears the prisoners saying their prayers together. Sometimes, they sing songs of faith and hope.

Here, in prison, he is exercising his faculties as a priest and, in his heart, he secretly prays "that such a life might continue forever."

"A sad group of men"

During his long journey from Portugal, Rodrigues had written back to his superiors of the worries that he and his colleagues had about being able to reach Japan and minister to the people there, about being able to succeed at their daunting assignment. "We priests are in some ways a sad group of men. Born into the world to render service to mankind, there is no one more wretchedly alone than the priest who does not measure up to his task."

From a hut in the hillside woods above Tomogi, he and Father Francis Garrpe had brought the sacraments to the villagers, and Rodrigues had reported back to Europe how he was filled with joy because he was "of some use to the people of this country at the ends of the earth...." But it was a tightly constrained ministry, always under the threat of persecution.

Now, in prison, of all places, he feels that he is fully a priest. Yet even as he preaches that God will not abandon believers, he is deeply troubled in his own soul, finding it more and more difficult to pray.

When first captured, Rodrigues had told one of his captors to put him to the test. But the official had only smiled and said that the Japanese authorities had learned their lesson. Martyring the priest would just make the peasants more obdurate. Rather than make the missionaries martyrs, the persecution now was directed at the lay Christians. They were undergoing horrors and death — but only as long as the priest refused to renounce his faith. If he gave in, if he apostatized, they would be spared.

In shock, the priest had begun the rosary, using his fingers, but the Our Fathers and Hail Marys were "empty and hollow." It wasn't until he pictured Jesus going through a similar imprisonment that his prayer became sincere. Now his life in prison is oddly serene. He is able to minister to the Christian captives. But, still, he has difficulty lifting his heart to God. At one point, he realizes that he has been forgetting to pray. But when he tries, the prayer that rises within him isn't one of thanksgiving but of petition, complaint, and resentment.

Later, after witnessing the beheading of Chokichi, Rodrigues attempts to recite the hymn "Hail, O Star of the Ocean," a plea to Mary the mother of Jesus, but he can't because to his mind comes the image of the one-eyed man's body being dragged across the courtyard, spilling red-black blood on the ground.

On the night his faith is put to its greatest test, Rodrigues hears Kichijiro in the courtyard, yelling his confession and seeking forgiveness. With a bitter bile in his mouth, the priest mumbles the words to absolve his betrayer, but his blessing doesn't come from the depth of his soul. He is still resentful of the man he calls his Judas.

He gives absolution "out of a sense of priestly duty."

QUESTIONS FOR REFLECTION OR DISCUSSION

Rodrigues feels that he is finally about to carry out the role of a priest when he is put in prison. What does this say about his concept of being a priest? His visits to the Christian prisoners are a way for prison authorities to keep them docile. In ministering to them, is Rodrigues in effect working for the officials? Explain your answer.

The psalm that Rodrigues recites to the other prisoners includes this assertion: "Blessed are the dead who die in the Lord." What does this line from Scripture say to you?

What does it mean when Rodrigues prays that his life in prison "might continue forever"? He says that priests who aren't able to be of service to humanity are "a sad group of men." He grants absolution to Kichijiro only "out of priestly duty." What does this say about the state of his own soul? Why? Name a priest whom you admire and describe why you do.

Why does Rodrigues have a difficult time praying after his capture? Why is his prayer "empty and hollow"? Why do his prayers turn to complaint and resentment? Does this ever happen to you? Give an example.

How would you describe Rodrigues' priestly faith? In what ways is his faith similar or different from your own?

CHAPTER NINE
RODRIGUES AND THE PASSION OF JESUS

Often throughout the novel *Silence*, Father Sebastian Rodrigues compares his sufferings and travails to those of Jesus.

This begins from the first moments that Rodrigues and Father Francis Garrpe spend on Japanese soil. As they hide in the dark along the shore hoping to avoid detection, the two priests wonder if they, like Jesus in the Garden of Gethsemane, will be betrayed. Will soldiers come with lanterns in the night to take them away to martyrdom? Will they, like Christ, need to entrust themselves "without reserve to the hands of men"?

But the two priests are not betrayed. Instead, they are delivered to the local Christians by the fisherman Kichijiro, a man they consider untrustworthy.

Ultimately, Kichijiro does prove to be treacherous, betraying Rodrigues weeks later to a group of soldiers who take the priest to a nearby village. There, he trembles in fear and misery. To settle himself, he calls to mind "a man who had been dragged from the Garden of Gethsemane to the palace of Caiphas."

Rodrigues closely identifies with the Galilean — but in a telling way. He does not see himself as being like the Jesus who preached from one end of Judea to the other, dealing with knotty moral questions. Nor the Jesus who told stories about Good Samaritans and wedding feasts. Nor the Jesus who comforted — and even cured and resurrected — those afflicted by the tragedies of life. No, the priest sees himself as being like Jesus in one way only — the Lord's passion and death.

To be fair, Rodrigues has lived his entire time in Japan under the threat of discovery, torture, and execution. Yet even in his letters back to Europe, he doesn't mention Jesus as a model when he describes his priestly work among the villagers of Tomogi and on the island of Fukazawa. Perhaps he expects that his superiors will take that as a given: Of course he's acting like Jesus in his missionary work!

Or maybe his emphasis on Christ's sufferings and crucifixion is an outgrowth of his long-held dream of a "glorious martyrdom," more evidence of his desire to be a hero and become a saint, entering heaven as the angels blast their trumpets. In prison, he imagines his future martyrdom and recalls what happened when Jesus died on the cross — how "from the temple had issued three bugle calls, one long, one short, and then one long again," how the sky had grown dark and the sun had disappeared and the veil of the temple was torn from top to bottom. This, writes Shusaku Endo, "was the image of martyrdom [Rodrigues] had long entertained."

What's also noteworthy is that Rodrigues has a tendency to see his own experiences — certainly fearful and fear-inducing — as equal in depth and intensity to the suffering of Jesus, even though his are often much less severe. For instance, while riding in a rowboat to find a new hiding place, he is thirsty and sucks salty sea water off his fingers while thinking of "Christ nailed to the Cross and the taste of vinegar in his mouth."

"Suffering that I now endure"

Endo writes that Jesus in the Garden of Gethsemane comes to the priest's mind twice while he is being held in prison, both in the deep dark of night.

The first time is shortly after he has watched Father Francis Garrpe and the three lay Christians die in the waters offshore. These deaths, together with the beheading of the one-eyed man, have shaken Rodrigues to the core. In his cell, he is listless and despairing. The guards have been drinking and laughing and clinking cups of sake. The priest squats in his cell, feeling alone and lonely. He envisions Jesus crouching similarly in Gethsemane, sweating blood and saying, "My soul is sorrowful even unto death."

On another night when Rodrigues is feeling even more alone and starkly isolated, he hears a sound that he takes to be the snoring of a drunken guard — the "kind of fellow who had killed" Jesus. The priest beats against the wall to protest the irritating noise, but the guards, "like those disciples who in Gethsemane slept in utter indifference to the torment of that man," don't respond.

When he equates his torments with those of Jesus, Rodrigues includes his trials before the samurai, particularly Inoue, the Governor of Chikugo. Preparing for one interrogation, he "dramatically" visualizes that it will be "like the meeting of Pilate and Christ." In his mind's eye, he sees a confused Pilate and a Jesus who is silent. Then, when he is squatting uncomfortably in the sand of the prison courtyard, awaiting the arrival of a panel of officials, he believes that the guard looking at him sees a man who looks as "Christ must have looked at the time of the scourging he endured."

Rodrigues, however, hasn't been scourged and isn't facing the imminent threat of scourging. He's just being forced to wait in a position that as a European he finds awkward, and he is sweating freely. When the officials do arrive, he is *not* silent. He engages in a debate under the seemingly encouraging eye of an old samurai with a smile that seems kind. It is a debate he feels he is winning at every turn — until he goes too far.

Afterward, Rodrigues remembers the smiling Inoue, and the memory brings to his mind the image of Jesus being whipped while Herod ate at a table decorated with flowers. Herod is also in his thoughts when he feels worn out by the frequent questioning he must endure. It is "the same old questions" from officials who, "like Herod when he faced Christ," aren't interested in the answers.

There is a parallel as well in the mind of Rodrigues between his own experience and the way the crowd treated Jesus as Pilate decided his fate. The crowd in Jerusalem, as the priest imagines it, greeted Christ "with shrieks and howls of anger." This he associates with how the crowd deals with him when he is led on a horse through Nagasaki. However, the people he sees aren't shrieking or howling at him. They're just curious, staring at him from "faces with those protruding teeth."

In the midst of his guards on another trip on horseback, Rodrigues sees farmers run to the roadside to gape at him. He thinks again of what Jesus went through: "Many centuries ago, that man tasted with his dried and swollen tongue all the suffering that I now endure.... And this sense of suffering shared softly eased his mind and heart more than the sweetest water."

"An unfortunate puppet?"

For all his identification with Christ's passion, Rodrigues is deeply troubled by one part of the story — the role of Judas, the apostle who betrayed Jesus.

The priest, of course, has his own betrayer in Kichijiro, a man whom Rodrigues despises from the moment they meet. Knowing little about his history, the Jesuit dismisses the Japanese as a "cowardly weakling." Even so, Kichijiro is the only guide that Rodrigues and Garrpe can find to take them into Japan. Faced with that fact, Rodrigues laughs silently with contempt at their need for Kichijiro.

From that moment, Rodrigues expects to suffer betrayal by Kichijiro. The priest and the peasant even talk about this possibility when Rodrigues discovers Kichijiro — "like a wild dog" — following him in the mountain forest.

Kichijiro whines to the priest, asking him to walk slower and to tell him where he's going. Then he says that the magistrate is offering a reward of three hundred pieces of silver to whoever turns in a priest.

"'So my price is three hundred pieces of silver,'" Rodrigues notes. "These were my first words to Kichijiro, and as I spoke them a bitter laugh crossed my face. Judas had sold Our Lord for thirty pieces of silver; I was worth ten times as much."

When Rodrigues awakens the next morning, he is surprised that he remains at liberty. He can't imagine why Kichijiro didn't sell him overnight for all that silver. Nonetheless, he is certain that he will be given over to the authorities, and like Jesus he wants to tell Kichijiro, "What thou do, do quickly."

As the two men move through the forest, the priest is lost in thought about what Jesus meant by those words — whether he was angry or resentful, whether somehow they were an expression of his love for the disciple. To save the world, did Jesus allow one man "to fall into eternal damnation"? Did he pray for Judas? Why didn't he stop Judas? Why didn't he save Judas?

These are thoughts Rodrigues has had most of his life, and even in the seminary no one he asked could give him a satisfactory answer. None of it made sense. Judas, it seemed to him, was nothing more than "an unfortunate puppet for the glory of that drama which was the life and death of Christ."

Rodrigues is thirsty. Kichijiro says he will go to get the priest a pitcher of water. When he returns, he is not alone. There are soldiers with him who take the priest into custody. "Father, forgive me," his betrayer says.

On the journey to prison, Rodrigues is hungry and exhausted; when the samurai stop for lunch, they simply tie him to a tree. Then a broken bowl of rice is put into his hands. He looks up, and there is Kichijiro. Rodrigues eats the rice, but he feels only anger toward his betrayer.

Yes, he reminds himself at another time, Jesus "searched out the ragged and the dirty...people with no attraction, no beauty." That is true love; the Jesuit knows that. Nonetheless, he is unable to forgive

Kichijiro, even if he does later give him absolution in the sacrament of Confession.

For all of his identification with Jesus, Rodrigues is clear about his feelings toward Kichijiro. For the Japanese peasant, the priest feels nothing but disgust. He finds him physically repugnant. He feels for him "a black and cruel emotion...from the very depths of his being."

Maybe, the priest thinks, that is what Jesus felt toward Judas. Even so, how could Jesus reject his betrayer? How could he cast him aside?

"Wasn't Judas no more than a puppet made use of for that man's crucifixion?"

QUESTIONS FOR REFLECTION OR DISCUSSION

Why does Rodrigues spend so much time thinking that his own sufferings are like those of Jesus? Do you ever do this? Why or why not? Why doesn't Rodrigues compare his experiences as a preacher, minister, or comforter with those of Jesus? Do you ever do this? Why or why not?

Why does Rodrigues equate the Japanese people "with those protruding teeth" who silently gape at him with the crowds in Jerusalem who directed angry shrieks and howls at Jesus? Why couldn't Rodrigues feel comfortable with the "ragged and dirty" as Jesus did? Do you ever have trouble with this? Tell a story, if you can.

Twice in the novel, Rodrigues wonders if Judas wasn't so much a sinner as "an unfortunate puppet for the glory of that drama which was the life and death of Christ." What do you think about Judas? Do you ever wonder why he really betrayed Jesus? If so, what reasons do you come up with?

Why is Rodrigues so angry at Kichijiro, even when he's not sure if Jesus was angry at Judas? How much is Kichijiro like and unlike Judas? Do the actions and thoughts of Kichijiro give you a new insight into the mind of Judas? What is it?

What does Rodrigues' identification with the passion of Jesus say about his faith? In what ways is his faith similar or different from your own?

CHAPTER TEN
RODRIGUES AND THE SILENCE OF GOD

It is mid-August. Father Sebastian Rodrigues has been in Japan for a little more than three months. He has ministered in secret to the Christians of a small village while hiding out in a hut in the wooded hills, and he has visited those at an island hamlet. Fearing capture, he has wandered desolate forests. He has been betrayed.

In captivity, he has seen Christians undergo hellish tortures and suffer martyrdom for their faith. But no physical sufferings have been inflicted on him. His has been instead a psychological torment, aimed at breaking his spirit and destroying his faith. In these agonies, he has seen himself as Christ-like, identifying himself with Jesus as he endured his great passion.

Rodrigues sees Jesus "crouching on the ashen earth of a Gethsemane that has imbibed all the heat of the day," abandoned by his clueless disciples, asleep nearby. Isolated and desolate, Jesus says, "My soul is sorrowful even unto death."

Did Jesus tremble with fear? Did Jesus feel abandoned by God? The priest shakes his head, trying to chase these questions from his mind.

On the cross, Jesus says, "*Eloi, Eloi, lama sabachthani?*" Those are Aramaic words that mean: "My God, my God, why have you forsaken me?" They come from Psalm 22: "My God, my God, why have you forsaken me? Why are you so far from helping me, from the words of my groaning? O my God, I cry by day, but you do not answer; and by night, but find no rest."

Rodrigues had often thought of those words on the cross as a prayer, but now he fears that they "issued from terror at the silence of God."

Was Jesus abandoned? Does God even exist? Has Rodrigues been wasting his life to promote a faith that is a wisp of nothing? Did the European missionaries and Japanese martyrs die for nothing? Did Jesus die for nothing?

As he often does in Shusaku Endo's novel *Silence*, the priest laughs bitterly, sourly. There is no humor to his laugh. It is a form of sobbing. As a child, thinking of God had brought him feelings of harmony and joy, but now God has become "an object of fear and perplexity."

In his anger and fear at the silence of God, Rodrigues is an echo of Job in the Bible.

"Why has Deus Sama given us this trial?"

In the Bible, the Book of Job stands apart as something very different from all the others — different in a scary way, in an unsettling way, in a faith-shaking way. It's in the Old Testament, but most scholars believe Job is a Gentile. For thousands of years, it's been a cliché to talk about the "patience of Job." The reality is, though, that Job isn't patient at all. He complains long and loudly to God.

Like the writer of Psalm 22, Job wants to know why there is pain and suffering in the world for those who are blameless. Why is there evil? Why is there death? These are questions at the core of human existence. Job demands answers from God.

In the 2,500-year-old Book of Job, the central character is a rich man who is a devout and upright believer in God. But, up in heaven, one of the multitudes in attendance to the Most High — a being called a "satan" (an adversary, a kind of prosecuting attorney) who, in many interpretations, is identified as *the* Satan — tells the Lord that Job is only devout and upright because he's received so many blessings.

This satan argues that Job will curse the Lord — that he will deny God, renounce God — if he loses his blessings. So, as a test, God gives the satan permission to afflict the faithful follower in any way, except taking his life. The satan kills all of Job's children and wipes away his wealth. Job responds: "The Lord has given, and the Lord takes away."

Then, the satan inflicts a terrible disease upon Job. But still the man remains steadfast in his faith in God. Then, a new worse affliction arrives — three friends who, in their turn, tell Job that he must be a great sinner to have suffered so much at God's hand. They are parroting the religious "wisdom" that many spiritual leaders have preached since the dawn of time.

Job, knowing his innocence, complains to God about his treatment, raising pointed questions about why God treats a good man in such a way. But he stops short of cursing the Lord. Instead, he curses the day he was born.

Ignoring the questions — or maybe not — God responds "from the whirlwind," telling Job that he doesn't and can't understand a Being who could create the world in all its array and beauty and complexity. It is a response that isn't exactly an answer. Yet, Job accepts it and stays steadfast in his belief.

In *Silence*, Christians, particularly Rodrigues, are in the role of Job. Like Job, Christian missionaries and their followers in Japan were once showered with rich blessings and great honors, as Rodrigues often recalls ruefully. Then, suddenly, the attitude of authorities radically shifted. The Christians were the same people they were before. They weren't doing anything differently. Now, though, instead of being esteemed, they were outlaws. They were hunted down, hideously tortured, and brutally executed.

Speaking for all of the Japanese Christians, Kichijiro asks Rodrigues why such suffering has come down upon them. Why is a Christian now forced to choose between being a martyr or an apostate? As the priest writes in a letter to his superiors, the young peasant stammers, "Why has Deus Sama given us this trial? We have done no wrong?"

Rodrigues has no warmth for Kichijiro, no compassion. He looks down on him, calls him a dog. Yet as he writes to the Jesuit leaders in Europe, he can't get the man's questions out of his mind and wonders, "Why had Our Lord imposed this torture and this persecution on poor Japanese peasants?"

Kichijiro's question, the priest writes, expresses a deeper one: Why has God remained silent?

"God with folded arms"

As the title *Silence* suggests, this question is at the center of Endo's novel and Rodrigues' crisis.

In Japan, Rodrigues lives in the heart of silence. Except for his short-lived companionable existence with Father Francis Garrpe in the hut above Tomogi, the priest is always alone, even when circumstances bring him into contact with others. He feels alien and set apart from everyone — from his persecutors; from his guards; from the crowds of gawkers who watch him move from one prison to another; from his former hero and now apostate Father Christovao Ferreira; from Kichijiro, the sniveling man he sees as a coward; and even from the other Christians in prison with him.

Isolated with his thoughts, Rodrigues experiences his prison as a place of silence that can be abruptly broken by "the angry barking voices of the guards" or by a sudden song from the cells of the other Christians: "We're on our way, we're on our way, we're on our way to the temple of Paradise."

Sometimes, this stillness has the element of boredom — the prison's "usual afternoon silence." More often, it is threatening — the "deathly silence" he experiences in his cell on the night of his great spiritual test. Many times, especially at moments of high stress, the silence of the priest's captivity is broken by the tedious, grinding, irritating insect rhythm of the cicada's mating call. It's a sound that seems to accentuate the silence. For Rodrigues, it carries no message and gives no answers.

Neither are there answers to be found in the silence of the rest of nature. When Mokichi and Ichizo are martyred on crosses in the rising and falling tide offshore, Rodrigues writes to his fellow Jesuits, "the sea which killed them surges on uncannily — in silence." Actually, the sea isn't silent. There is, he notes, the monotonous rolling of the waves but, as with the cicadas, this only heightens the lack of other sounds.

When one night he is brought into a town where Christians used to live, it is nothing but burning wreckage, leveled and abandoned. Not a soul moves. The countryside and the sea and the darkness itself are "silent as death."

But for Rodrigues, the greatest silence is the silence of God. While he is still in contact with Europe, he describes that silence in his final letter: "Behind the depressing silence of the sea, the silence of God... the feeling that while men raise their voices in anguish, God remains with folded arms, silent." Later, at every turn as a prisoner, Rodrigues finds himself confronted by this stillness, this emptiness.

He yearns for answers — and an end to the pain that he and the Christians are undergoing: "Why have you abandoned us so completely?...remained silent like the darkness that surrounds me? Why? At least tell me why. We are not strong men like Job who was afflicted with leprosy as a trial. There is a limit to our endurance. Give us no more suffering."

Preaching to the other Christians in the prison, the priest tells them that God won't remain silent. Yet, in his heart, he hears nothing. When Garrpe is asked to renounce his faith so that three lay Christians won't be drowned like "basket worms" in the sea, Rodrigues shouts inside his head, "Apostatize! Apostatize!" Unable to watch Garrpe's martyrdom, he turns away and reprimands God: "You are silent. Even in this moment are you silent?"

Again and again, he all but screams to heaven for God to speak — to take away the agony and explain why it even exists, why the innocent must suffer, why evil is in the world, why there is death.

On the night of his crisis of faith, just after Rodrigues has learned that what he has thought to be the irritating sound of a guard snoring is actually the agonized moans of Christians hanging over the pit, Ferreira tells the younger man that God will do nothing to save those who are suffering or to save him. But Rodrigues can act — he can end their pain by putting his foot on the image of Jesus, by trampling on the *fumi-e*.

The prisoner puts his fingers to his ears and pleads with God to break the silence — the silence that greeted the deaths of Mokichi and Ichizo, the silence that greeted the slaying of the one-eyed man, the silence that greeted the drowning deaths of Garrpe and the three Christians wrapped up like "basket worms."

And now — *now* — he again listens for an answer: "Why is God continually silent while those groaning voices go on?"

QUESTIONS FOR REFLECTION OR DISCUSSION

Rodrigues wonders if, in the Garden of Gethsemane and also on the cross, Jesus felt abandoned by God. Jesus says, "My God, my God, why have you forsaken me?" The priest had long thought of this as a prayer, but now he fears it is "terror at the silence of God." What do you think?

Rodrigues notes that, as a child, he saw God as a source of harmony and joy, but now God seems to be "an object of fear and perplexity." What are some of the ways you think about God, based on what is going on in your life at the time?

Kichijiro asks Rodrigues why God has given such trials to the Japanese Christians, especially when earlier God had blessed them so fruitfully. Rodrigues takes up that question in his letter to his superiors. How do you think they would have/should have answered him?

The priest experiences silence in the prison, in his cell, in the landscape, in the darkness of night, and in the mindlessness of the sea. This is his perception. Could others have different perceptions of these things? Explain your answer.

When Rodrigues thinks about the silence of God, he envisions God with folded arms. What does this say about his image of God? Do you ever experience God as being silent? Is God sometimes as silent for you as for Rodrigues? Give an example of this, if you can.

What does Rodrigues' focus on the silence of God say about his faith? In what ways is it similar or different from your own?

CHAPTER ELEVEN
RODRIGUES AND THE FACE OF JESUS

In prison, where he is able to minister to a handful of other Christian prisoners, Father Sebastian Rodrigues prays silently that his calm and contented life there will never end. He knows he is under threat of torture and death. He knows those other Christians are, too. Yet he finds these days filled with serenity. And when he does feel fear and anxiety, he calls to mind the face of Jesus.

This is a face that, from his childhood, has been "the fulfillment of his every dream and ideal." A beautiful face with "soft, clear eyes," the face he imagines that was seen by those at the Sermon at the Mount. A face that, even during the agonizing tortures that Jesus underwent, never lost its loveliness.

Rodruiges' thoughts of the face of Jesus comfort him.

"His beautiful face"

Earlier in Shusaku Endo's novel *Silence*, Rodrigues has written home to his Jesuit superiors that the root of his fascination with the face of Jesus is the fact that the Bible says nothing about how the Savior looked. It's left to his imagination.

In one letter, he notes that early Christians pictured Jesus as having a gentle countenance. But, then — the priest writes disapprovingly — the Eastern Church gave the Lord "the long nose, the curly hair, the black beard...of an oriental Christ." He's more accepting of how, in the Middle Ages, artists painted Jesus with a king's majesty.

The image that Rodrigues prefers above all others, however, is in "The Resurrection," a fresco by the Renaissance artist Piero della Francesca in the palace of the painter's Italian hometown of Sansepolcro, which was named for the Holy Sepulchre where the body of Jesus was entombed. In the fresco, the newly resurrected Jesus stands, half in and half out of the tomb, looking directly at the viewer.

It is, for Rodrigues, a face that exudes "vigor and strength" and a face that features "the expression of encouragement it had when he commanded his disciples three times, 'Feed my lambs, feed my lambs, feed my lambs.'" And unblushingly the priest writes to his superiors that he is "fascinated by the face of Christ just like a man fascinated by the face of his beloved."

He repeats this in another letter: "From childhood I have clasped that face to my breast just like the person who romantically idealizes the countenance of one he loves. While I was still a student, studying in the seminary, if ever I had a sleepless night, his beautiful face would rise up in my heart."

Rodrigues pictures this "beautiful face" as having clear blue eyes, tranquil features, and a look of trust.

While wandering in the mountains, afraid of being captured and tortured, Rodrigues squats by a pool of water and looks down to see his own face reflected, a face covered with mud and stubble, "the face of a haunted man filled with uneasiness and exhaustion."

It is then he thinks of Jesus, but not the Jesus who is suffering as Rodrigues is now. It is the idealized Jesus of his dreams: "This was the face of a crucified man, a face which for so many centuries had given inspiration to artists. This man none of these artists had seen with his own eyes, yet they portrayed his face — the most pure, the most beautiful that had claimed the prayers of man and has corresponded with his highest aspirations." Indeed, Rodrigues is certain that "his real face was more beautiful than anything they have envisaged."

For him, the face of Jesus isn't static. At many points in the novel, it communicates comfort, support, and even mild rebuke to the priest. For instance, Rodrigues sees the encouraging face of Jesus in a shadow on the wall of his cell following his debate with the panel of samurais that ended with them laughing at him. The shadow seems to form into the eyes of the Lord, looking directly at him. He imagines the rest of the face, and it gives him a feeling that he has done well in the debate. He glows "with pride like a child."

At another time, however, when Rodrigues realizes that he isn't able to love the poor and outcasts as Jesus had, the Lord's face comes into his mind, this time weeping. It leaves the priest feeling ashamed.

And he feels chastised by the face that he imagines on the night when he is to be put to the ultimate test — a face that is drawn and emaciated, the face of the suffering Jesus, the patient Jesus, the Jesus who looks on the priest with sorrow. "When you suffer," the face seems to say, "I suffer with you. To the end I am close to you."

A few moments later, Rodrigues hears what he takes to be the snoring of a guard nearby. He bitterly dismisses the man as crude and cruel. The guard, he thinks to himself, is exactly the sort who killed "the man whose face was the best and the most beautiful that ever one could dream of."

QUESTIONS FOR REFLECTION OR DISCUSSION

From childhood, the face of Jesus is "the fulfillment of his every dream and ideal" for Rodrigues. Do you have the same emotional attachment to the physical image of Christ? Was Jesus beautiful? Explain.

Why was Rodrigues disapproving of the Eastern Church's image of "an oriental Christ"? Do you share this feeling? Why or why not?

After his debate with Inoue and the samurais, Rodrigues sees the face of Jesus in a shadow on the wall of his cell. And, feeling approval from the face, he glows "with pride like a child." How childlike is Rodrigues? Twice, Rodrigues compares his devotion to the face of Jesus with the way a person "romantically idealizes the countenance of one he loves." What do you think of that?

His imagining of the face of Jesus can make Rodrigues feel shame. Nonetheless, even on the night of his ultimate test of faith, he thinks of that face as "the best and the most beautiful that ever one could dream of." Why do you think the priest emphasizes so strongly what he imagines to be the physical beauty of Jesus?

What does Rodrigues' obsession with the face of Jesus say about his faith? In what ways is his faith similar or different from your own?

PART THREE
FAITH

I fled Him, down the nights and down the days;
I fled Him, down the arches of the years;
I fled Him, down the labyrinthine ways
Of my own mind; and in the mist of tears
I hid from Him, and under running laughter.

"THE HOUND OF HEAVEN," FRANCIS THOMPSON

CHAPTER TWELVE
THE VOICE OF GOD

Father Sebastian Rodrigues, with his many flaws and blind-spots, is one of us. He wants to do good but is overwhelmed by the complexities of his life. He dreams of being great, but he is weak and fragile, like all of us.

The priest is a lot like his Judas, the peasant Kichijiro, a man he detests as a contemptible, foul-smelling drunk who, as Rodrigues sees it, goes through life like a scared mouse or a pig rooting in its own vomit. Kichijiro knows his own failings and tells the priest that not everyone is strong enough to be a martyr. He says that he would be a perfect Christian and go to heaven if he lived in an era when believers weren't being persecuted. And Rodrigues, despite his disgust toward the man, realizes that what he says is true.

It's also true for Rodrigues.

Callow and emotionally unformed

Rodrigues is a young priest, callow and emotionally unformed, just out of the seminary with little or no pastoral experience under his belt. He has been trained to serve a parish or teach theology. He has been trained to enter a world where he would be respected for his learning and honored for his vocation, a Christian world, a world in which the Catholic Church is a center of power and might.

Rodrigues is filled with idealistic illusions, like any newly ordained priest — indeed, like any young man or woman entering upon a career. If he had followed the usual path of a priest and a Jesuit, he would have gone through some everyday, real-world experiences to temper those dreams.

Instead, he and two similarly untested friends wheedle permission to take the arduous and dangerous 15,000-mile sea journey to Japan on a quest to find out what happened to their beloved and respected teacher, Father Christovao Ferreira. After decades of service to the Japanese, did he renounce his faith as the rumors reaching Europe say? Or did he die "a glorious martyrdom"?

In attempting to coax authorization from their superiors, the three young priests see the search to answer these questions as their primary task. The idea of ministering to the Japanese is mentioned only in passing.

In the end, just two of the Jesuits — Rodrigues and Father Francis Garrpe — are able to get into Japan. They attempt to support each other, but both are naïve and inexperienced. And they are faced with terrifying challenges. The cruel perils they confront would daunt even the most veteran missionary. Everything about Japan seems totally alien to them. All the certainties of their European existence are thrown into question. The clothing, the food, the odors, even the incessant sound of the cicadas disorient them.

In *Silence*, Shusaku Endo depicts Garrpe as an irritable questioner. He badgers Kichijiro about whether he is a Christian. He reacts with anger when two women giggle as they watch the two priests eat: "Are we so queer?" His outward actions give a glimpse into his inner perplexity.

For Rodrigues, the extreme foreignness of the life he finds in Japan "at the ends of the earth" leaves him befuddled and demoralized, as he acknowledges in his letters back to Europe. He is in Japan ostensibly to serve the embattled Christian community, but his reaction to his flock is often a bitter laugh at their odd names; at their blank, seemingly identical faces; at their mumbling attempts to pronounce Portuguese and Latin words. He sees them as monkeys and as mindless cattle. As he watches a baby being baptized, all he can think is that the child will live and die "like a beast."

Yet, time and again, the Japanese Christians show themselves to be courageous in standing up for their faith and in dying for their beliefs. "We're on our way, we're on our way, we're on our way to the temple of Paradise," they sing.

Rodrigues is shocked by their deaths, shattered to his core. Nonetheless, even as they are martyred, the Jesuit finds fault with their image of heaven as a place where they will no longer be oppressed and no longer required to pay taxes. And he sees them as undergoing a martyrdom that is wretched and agonizing, far from glorious, far from the sort to evoke waves of trumpet blasts from God's holy hosts of angels.

The priest has no emotional connection to the Japanese people. He makes no friends. He is too much the European, and he looks down on the peasants, the guards, and even the magistrate Inoue, dismissing them as primitive. He is the sort of priest who, throughout the history of the Church, even today, defines his role as an instructor, confessor, and judge. His is a top-down understanding of faith. Community, especially community with this beast-like people, isn't part of the equation for Rodrigues.

In his mind, he has nothing to learn from the members of his flock. He is among them to give them the truth. That, though, is where he is brought up short.

In the Europe of this era, despite the fragmentation caused by the Protestant Reformation, nearly everyone (except for Jews and Muslims on the margins of society) lives inside the same Christian belief system. Yes, there are martyrs from each sect — decapitated, hanged, or burned at the stake for their understanding of Jesus' message, viewed as heretical by those who have a different understanding. Nonetheless, they all exist in the same culture, the same civilization, the same way of thinking.

But in Japan, Rodrigues finds a culture that is seemingly antithetical to the core message of Jesus. It is an ancient society with its own way of looking at life and its own sense of the spiritual. It is a proud and highly sophisticated civilization. Yet the European missionaries (and traders) come to the islands with great arrogance. One priest in the novel, for instance, actively ridicules young Japanese men who want to become priests, refusing to let them be ordained.

Inoue and Ferreira call Japan a "swamp" for Christianity. Despite their early openness to the missionaries, Japanese authorities now view this European-based faith as ill-fitted to the nation, seeking to expel it in the way a body tries to reject a transplanted heart.

Rodrigues experiences Japan as a place so foreign that it is as if it were another planet. Yet Inoue, the magistrate leading the persecutions, believes deeply in the Japanese way of life and way of thinking. He argues that, for *his* people, the missionaries and their teachings are what's alien.

Perhaps if Rodrigues had had more experience under his belt before travelling to Japan, he might have been better prepared for the culture shock of arriving in this Asian land in the midst of a persecution. Yet even his beloved teacher Ferreira, a veteran missionary if there ever was one, succumbs to the psychological pressure of his captivity and, by the time Rodrigues meets him, is parroting Inoue's assertions that Christianity never had a chance to take root in Japan.

Indeed Ferreira, like the magistrate, contends that the belief espoused by the Japanese Christians isn't Christianity at all but rather something warped and twisted into a deformed version of the faith.

Friendless, alone, isolated

When facing the ultimate test of his faith, Rodrigues is hamstrung by his youth and his lack of preparation. He is hampered by his European-centric world view and by his inability — and unwillingness — to reach out for support and encouragement from the Japanese lay Christians.

He fails himself as well.

From childhood, he has created a dream world in which missionaries are shining beacons of faith and, if challenged by persecution, endure torture and death with a haloed equanimity. It is a world embodied in the religious art of the time, a place where pain exists only as an irritation or not at all, a physical realm in which eyes are turned to heaven and the blessed succor of the heavenly host and the Beatific Vision of God.

This is the world of the "glorious martyrdom." But Rodrigues finds that it doesn't exist in the real world. Instead, the tortured deaths of Japanese Christians are ugly, brutal affairs. They are worn to death by the rising and the falling of the tide. They are tied up as "basket worms" and dumped into the sea to drown. They are decapitated with the single slice of a samurai's sword, leaving a trail of black-red blood in the sand of the courtyard.

There is no heavenly glow. And the irritating, machine-like cicadas continue to chitter.

Another aspect of this dream world is Rodrigues' out-of-kilter identification of himself with Jesus — not the Jesus who washed the feet of the disciples nor the Jesus who reached out to help those on the margins of society but the Jesus who underwent great tortures and, to the young priest's mind, suffered a glorious death.

Rodrigues wants to be a hero. He wants to be a saint. He wants to be Jesus. But he's playing a role. He is Rodrigues as priest, Rodrigues as Jesus. Not simply Rodrigues the human being. He has no psychological depth, no psychological center. And Inoue capitalizes on this. He and his deputies browbeat and brainwash the young Jesuit. They prey on the young man's insecurities. Rodrigues is a man whose life is built on a reliance on societal structures and on a dearly held trust in his own dreams. And those are all undermined by Inoue and his allies.

Rodrigues is left naked to face his ultimate test.

Friendless, alone, isolated, he turns to the face of Jesus, as he has all his life. In the image of that face, as it arises in his mind, he finds acceptance and encouragement and challenge and forgiveness — and always an other-worldly beauty. But that's not enough. Instead, the priest demands that God speak to him. This is the flipside to his complaints about the silence of God. Endo's novel *Silence* could just as well be titled *Speak!*

Like Job in the Bible, Rodrigues badgers God for answers. He wants to know why bad things are happening to him and the Japanese Christians. He wants to know why the innocent have to suffer and die. He wants to know that he is not alone.

Job never got a direct answer from God. Neither did the many saints, such as Thérèse of Lisieux, John of the Cross, and Mother Teresa, who all suffered a dark night of the soul when, at times in their lives, they felt abandoned by the Lord.

What Job did and what those saints did was to endure. This is the true meaning of the term "the patience of Job." Job wasn't patient in the sense of staying quiet. He loudly harangued God with his questions. But when the answers he sought weren't forthcoming, Job didn't turn his back on God. He recommitted himself to his faith and endured his pain and suffering. He stayed resolute in his faith, even though he could not feel God's comfort nor the joy of God's presence.

Great joy

On the night of his ultimate test, Rodrigues is weak, innocent, and emotionally frail. And he is being bullied into making what seems like a choice but, in many ways, isn't.

If the young Jesuit refuses to renounce his faith, other Christians will suffer and die. At this moment, some are hanging over the pit, slowly bleeding to death. If he stands fast, more will be tortured and killed.

If, instead, Rodrigues renounces his faith, he will turn his back on everything he has been taught and on every ideal he has held sacred. He will be disgraced. His superiors back in Europe will excommunicate him. Based on everything he has been taught, he will condemn himself to everlasting pain and anguish in hell.

Rodrigues has long dreamed of "a glorious martyrdom." But to his shock he has come to learn that undergoing cruel pain and death for the faith is a grisly, wretched torment.

If he steps on the image of Jesus, if he tramples on the *fumi-e*, he will send a signal to all Japanese Christians that such torment isn't worth the sacrifice. He will be saying that it is better for a Christian to renounce the faith than to suffer martyrdom. He will be saying that it is more important for believers to avoid suffering than to live out their beliefs at whatever the cost. Earlier, Rodrigues had said that even the last priest remaining in Japan would have "the same significance as a single candle burning in the catacombs." In trampling the *fumi-e*, he will be blowing out that candle.

This is no choice at all. Each option is devastating. And yet it is a real choice. He can't dodge the need to make a decision. And there will be consequences to his actions. He is being forced, in the real world, to take a stand.

In the dark of the darkest night of his soul, Rodrigues finally understands that the "snoring" he has been hearing and scoffing at is actually the moaning of those hanging over the pit. He tells Ferreira that these Christians will merit "a reward of eternal joy" for their sufferings. But the older man sneers that, by refusing to submit, Rodrigues is making himself and his reputation — and his salvation — of greater value than the lives of these peasants. "You dread to be the dregs of the Church," he tells the captive priest.

Jesus would not have been so confused, Ferreira says. "Certainly Christ would have apostatized for them." He says this three times.

Rodrigues screams to him to go away. But the door of the cell is opened, and his former teacher puts his hand on the young man's shoulder, telling him, "You are now going to perform the most painful act of love that has ever been performed." He says it a second time.

They walk down the corridor to where the interpreter stands with two guards. On the ground, the interpreter sets a large piece of wood, stained with dirt and blood. Attached to the wood is a small copper medal on which is engraved the face of Jesus, an engraving worn down and blurred by all the feet that have stepped on it.

This, though, isn't the glorified face of the Lord that Rodrigues has loved and cherished all his life — not the face filled with majesty, nor the face made lovely in the endurance of pain, nor the face that exudes strength and will. It is the sunken face of a man at the end of his rope. Here, the face of Jesus is ugly. His head is crowned with thorns. His thin arms are stretched out on the cross. "Courage," Ferreira says.

As Rodrigues looks down at the medal, he silently talks to Jesus about how, all his life and especially since coming to Japan, he has found strength and comfort in calling to his mind "the most beautiful, the most precious thing in the world" — the Lord's face. "It's only a formality," the interpreter says.

The young priest lifts his foot, feeling a blunt pain in the action. After feeling oppressed by the silence of God for such a long time, he now hears the voice of Jesus:

"Trample! Trample! I more than anyone know of the pain in your foot. Trample! It was to be trampled that I was born into this world. It was to share men's pain that I carried my cross."

And onto the medal with the face of Jesus, Rodrigues presses his foot. And the dawn breaks. And a cock crows.

And the young priest feels great joy.

"My faith is different"

In the final pages of *Silence*, Shusaku Endo tells this story three times — as it happens and then, twice, as Rodrigues recalls the terrible moment. Each account includes the words of Jesus telling the young man to trample the *fumi-e*.

The third time, though — when the now-disgraced priest has been approached, yet again, by Kichijiro for forgiveness — Rodrigues imagines a conversation with Jesus.

Rodrigues has already been placed under permanent house arrest. He has been given a Japanese name and a Japanese wife. He and Ferreira are working for Inoue to explain the significance of Christian objects that, despite the persecution of believers, are still finding their way into Japan. In identifying these, the two men are providing evidence to the authorities that likely will result in the torture and deaths of Christians.

Ferreira is Apostate Peter, and Rodrigues is Apostate Paul. Even the small children know this and taunt the two men with these names.

Kichijiro — the fearful, smelly peasant who betrayed the priest to the authorities — has come to his door to ask for absolution. "Father, I betrayed you. I trampled on the picture of Christ." In the past, the priest has treated his betrayer with contempt, but not now. Now he knows that he, too, has trampled on the *fumi-e*.

In recalling that terrible moment, Rodrigues hears Jesus tell him to put his foot on the worn-down copper etching, and he responds, "Lord, I resented your silence."

Jesus says he wasn't silent but that he stood and suffered with the young priest.

Rodrigues says that Jesus told Judas to go away. Why did he do that?

Jesus says he *didn't* tell Judas to go away. He says he told Judas the same thing he told Rodrigues.

Rodrigues looks at Kichijiro and tells him that he will give him absolution, but only because there is no other priest in Japan to hear his confession. He knows that the Church authorities in Europe would consider his action a sacrilege.

The priest tells himself that he is not an apostate. "Lord," he says in the depths of his heart, "you alone know that I did not renounce my faith." Nonetheless, the young man feels like a traitor, like a coward, and he sees Ferreira that way. He has contempt for his former teacher. He hates him and pities him, even as he recognizes that they are "two inseparable twins."

When he has a final meeting with Inoue, Rodrigues says that his fight wasn't really with the Japanese authorities but with his own concept of Christianity. The magistrate isn't so sure. He hears Rodrigues out and then asks him if he isn't just deluding himself. "You may deceive other people, but not me." After all, the magistrate says, the roots of Christianity in Japan have been cut because Rodrigues and other priests have chosen to deny their faith rather that stand fast.

He tells the priest that he has questioned other missionaries about the difference between the mercy that the Christian God bestows and the mercy that comes from Buddha. The best answer, he says, came from one priest who said that the Christian can't just rely on God but also must retain a strong heart. The willingness to apostatize, the magistrate implies, is proof that the missionaries in Japan lost that strong heart — proof that their faith was distorted by the swamp of Japan. "The Christianity you brought to Japan has changed its form and has become a strange thing."

Rodrigues can't be sure that Inoue isn't right. He wonders if all his protestations that he still loves Jesus are just a cover for his own weakness. He is, after all, no different from Kichijiro. And he knows that now "my Lord is different from the God that is preached" back in Europe. "My faith," he prays to Jesus, "is different from what it was; but I love you still."

But he spends the rest of his life feeling shame and guilt.

QUESTIONS FOR REFLECTION OR DISCUSSION

How well do you think Father Sebastian Rodrigues understands himself? What sort of a priest would he have been if he had stayed in Europe? Why do you think so? What could Rodrigues or his superiors have done to better prepare for coming to Japan?

Like Job in the Bible, Rodrigues castigates God for being silent in the face of the great persecution that he and the Japanese Christians are undergoing. How much is he like Job? And how much not like Job? How much are you like or unlike both of them?

Rodrigues hears the voice of Jesus telling him to "Trample!" on the fumi-e. And, when he does, he feels great joy. Why? Why isn't the joy that he feels at the moment of stepping on the image of Jesus more long-lasting? Why does he hate Ferreira and himself so much?

Inoue thinks the young priest is deceiving himself about his decision to step on the image of Jesus. Rodrigues recognizes that the magistrate may be right. In his heart, though, he tells Jesus that his faith is different now but that his love for the Lord is still strong. What do you think? How do you feel?

After finishing Endo's novel, list three or more words that describe you own faith. Share them with others if you can.

CONCLUSION

Shusaku Endo's 1966 novel *Silence* is a great work of world literature because it raises questions. Endo asks great, deep, troubling questions of Rodrigues — and, by extension, of his readers. And he leaves it to those readers to provide the answers.

Does this mean he's a weak author, afraid to take a stand? Or is it a courageous act?

I see Endo as courageous, in the same way that William Shakespeare and Leo Tolstoy and the author of the Book of Job were courageous in facing the unanswerable questions of human life.

Was Father Sebastian Rodrigues right to put his foot on the etched face of Jesus — to ritually renounce his faith — in order to save the lives of Japanese Christians?

Should he have stood firm for his faith regardless of the costs to him and others?

In trampling on the *fumi-e* was the young priest saying that all of the Japanese Christians — as well as all martyrs throughout history — had died in vain?

Or was he saying that, in the face of oppression and persecution, it is the duty of the believer to do whatever possible to ease suffering?

Is Rodrigues really hearing the voice of Jesus? Or is he fooling himself?

Throughout human history, believers have given their lives for their faith. They have refused to buckle under to torture and threats and have gone — at times even joyfully — to their deaths. Today, in some parts of the world, Christians are being killed every day for believing in Jesus.

Indeed, there would be no Christianity if Jesus, the first martyr, hadn't died on the cross. And there would be no Christianity if believers in every era hadn't stood fast.

Faith is only real if it results in action.

If, in our lives, faith is simply something that makes us feel warm and fuzzy and comfortable, it's not faith. As Pope Francis has said throughout his papacy, Christianity demands each believer to reach out to others, especially those on the margins of society. To form community with them. To help and be helped.

This can mean standing up for the faith, regardless of the cost. It can also mean doing whatever is possible to relieve suffering. Is one choice always better than the other?

Like Rodrigues, we are all weak. Yet we have to confront the challenges that arise in our lives. Each day, there are choices that have to be made. Each day, we are tested by realities out of our control. Still, we are called to respond in one way or another.

Can you read *Silence* and know — really know — which choice Rodrigues should have made? Can you come away from the book being certain that the young priest was right — or wrong — in how he chose?

I can't.

Endo's novel is not about judgment. It is about recognizing that faith isn't easy. Nor is it simple.

It is about the doubt that is at the heart of faith. There is no certainty to faith. There is only the leap that the believer makes — a choice to believe despite doubt, despite the lack of proof, despite outside pressures. There is only the decision to accept a way of life — and live it.

Silence is filled with believers. It is filled with faith — and with the pain and the questions that are part and parcel with faith.

It is filled with the mystery that is faith, a mystery for which each of us must find our own answers.

We are all Rodrigues.

APPENDIX

LISTENING TO SILENCE: OTHER PERSPECTIVES

I find Shusaku Endo's *Silence* a disconcerting masterpiece, and so do most commentators.

In his 2001 survey of important religious writing, *Dante to "Dead Man Walking": One Reader's Journey through the Christian Classics*, Father Raymond A. Schroth, a Jesuit, calls *Silence* "one of the most depressing novels I have ever read. But I've read it three times."

In another compilation, *One Hundred Great Catholic Books: From Early Centuries to the Present* (2007), Don Brophy writes that the myriad complex questions that Endo raises make his book "a disturbing and memorable reading experience."

Such lists have helped raise the novel's profile. In 1999, for instance, *Silence* was named by the publishing house HarperCollins as one of the "100 Best Spiritual Books of the Twentieth Century."

Even more important, though, was the book's inclusion on a much shorter list — the list that Graham Greene gave of the three best novels he'd read in 1976. He called *Silence*, "one of the finest novels of our time."

A few years later, in the United States, Endo's book got a strong boost from another major writer, John Updike. Writing in *The New Yorker*, Updike called the novel "a remarkable work, a somber, delicate, and startlingly empathetic study" of Rodrigues and his test of faith.

The New Yorker was also the setting in 1989 when poet-novelist Brad Leithauser said, "In moral terms, *Silence* is as complex and instructive as almost any novel I know."

Betrayal or sacrifice?

Widely praised as a great work of literature, *Silence* has sparked myriad interpretations.

For instance, upon its initial publication in Japan in 1966, the novel was denounced by Japanese Catholic leaders as an "aesthetic glorification of apostasy," notes Van C. Gessel in an essay, "*Silence* on Opposite Shores" in the 2015 book *Approaching "Silence": New Perspectives on Shusaku Endo's Classic Novel*, edited by Mark W. Dennis and Darren J. N. Middleton. One priest even suggested that the novel reads as if it were "an affirmation of, even an exhortation to, apostasy."

Nonetheless, *Silence* was a Japanese bestseller in large part because, Gessel writes, it was adopted by non-Christian, college-age leftists who saw it as an allegory on recent history. Thirty years earlier, their socialist predecessors had sought to bring Marxism into Japan, only to be persecuted, tortured, and sometimes killed for their beliefs.

Gessel, a professor of Japanese at Brigham Young University in Provo, Utah, writes that in the West *Silence* is seen as "the antithesis of Arthur Miller's *The Crucible* in which John Proctor chooses death over betraying the values he holds sacred."

Prominent religious historian Garry Wills wrote in a 1981 review of seven of Endo's books in the *New York Review of Books* that *Silence* bears a great resemblance to Greene's 1940 novel *The Power and the Glory* — with one major difference: "The whiskey priest of *The Power and the Glory* does not defect or lose his faith; he maintains a priestly ministry despite his own unworthiness, which partially qualifies him for serving other weak people. Endo explores a more interesting paradox; his priest does defect, not from weakness but from love, to spare Christian converts the persecution mounted against them."

Even so, it is possible to see Rodrigues as a weak man who followed an easier path by apostatizing. Gessel, however, strongly disagrees: "Endo's vital point that Rodrigues, in debasing himself and making of himself a sacrifice because of his intense love for others, is performing the most Christ-like of the options...placed before him."

Growth, change, and mother-love

Indeed, Gessel argues that "Rodrigues's act of love" is evidence of "his true conversion" in the act of trampling the *fumi-e*. This is an analysis that is often echoed in one way or another by commentators.

John Kaltner, a professor of Muslim-Christian relations at Rhodes College in Memphis, Tennessee, and another essayist in the *Approaching "Silence"* anthology, writes that in stepping on the image of Jesus the young priest "simultaneously violates his priestly duties and lives out the gospel message."

In fact, in his essay "'Silence' in the Classroom," Kaltner argues that Rodrigues is "a paradigm of growth and change" for people today.

Writing along the same lines in the anthology, Christopher B. Wachal, an English professor at Marquette University in Milwaukee, author of "Forbidden Ships to Chartered Tours: Endo, Apostasy, and Globalization," asserts: "My contention here is that we must understand apostasy as a transgression of traditional Western Christian teaching and as a means of entry into a new form of Christian life annexed and adapted to this context."

The novel, in other words, tells a story of "finding faith in one's weakest moments."

American Christian writer Philip Yancey asserts in his 1995 book *The Jesus I Never Knew* that Endo's novel is based on the novelist's belief that "Jesus brought the message of mother-love to balance the father-love of the Old Testament."

Yancey expands on that in his introduction to the 2016 book-long meditation on the novel by noted artist Makoto Fujimura titled *Silence and Beauty*. He writes that the failure of Christianity to convert many

Japanese is because of "the Western emphasis on God's fatherhood," and he goes on: "Mother love tends to be unconditional, accepting the child no matter what, regardless of behavior. Father love tends to be more provisional, bestowing approval as the child measures up to certain standards of behavior.... For Christianity to have any appeal to the Japanese, Endo suggests, it must stress instead the mother love of God, the love that forgives wrongs and binds wounds and draws, rather than forces, others to itself."

Director Martin Scorsese, who recently directed a film version of *Silence*, sees the book as an examination of belief and doubt. In the Foreword in a new edition of the novel published by Picador Modern Classics, he writes: "Questioning may lead to great loneliness, but if it co-exists with faith — true faith, abiding faith — it can end in the most joyful sense of communion. It's this painful, paradoxical passage — from certainty to doubt to loneliness to communion — that Endo understands so well, and renders so clearly, carefully, and beautifully in *Silence*."

Ground Zero realities and a Holy Saturday author

Yet, is it all so clear?

Was Rodrigues so sure of his decision? Was he happy with it? Did he feel encircled and comforted by the mother love of God? Did he feel a sense of communion?

I don't think so. If this is a true conversion, it's highly unusual.

To be sure, Endo describes the young priest as being filled with joy after stepping on the dirty, worn image of Jesus. But this joy doesn't seem to last. The tone of the rest of the book is decidedly depressed. In the aftermath of his act, Rodrigues seems traumatized, and the trauma appears to continue to the end of his life. He's not sure about his motivations nor about whether he's done the right thing.

I think the artist Fujimura is onto something when he writes: "Reading Endo is like reading a mystery novel in which many of the clues prove to misdirect the reader. When Endo published *Silence*, some religious authorities wanted to ban their parishioners from reading the book; this turned out to reveal Endo's scheme to take readers into some of these embedded mysteries. I believe Endo anticipated — even welcomed — those negative responses. They serve as a way to expose the dark realities behind religious convictions, and ultimately they cause us to experience more deeply, through his books, the presence of grace in dark, traumatic times."

For Fujimura, *Silence* is "about facing the Ground Zero realities of any age and in any culture." (Nagasaki, where Rodrigues lands and tries to minister to the underground Christian community, was also where the United States dropped the second atomic bomb at the end of World War II.)

Fujimura writes that Endo, as a novelist, is a "Holy Saturday author describing the darkness of waiting for Easter light to break into our world." He is a writer who practices "the art of brokenness."

Rodrigues lives a Holy Saturday life. So do all of us, broken and weak, looking, hoping, yearning for the Easter light. We are all trying, in our own awkward ways, to live our belief in the Resurrection.

ALSO AVAILABLE FROM ACTA PUBLICATIONS

SILENCE: A NOVEL
Shusaku Endo
214 pages, paperback

SILENCE AND BEAUTY:
HIDDEN FAITH BORN OF SUFFERING
Makoto Fujimura
264 pages, hardcover

LITERARY PORTALS TO PRAYER™

Each volume of this innovative series contains fifty prayer starters: excerpts from the works of cherished authors, poets, and playwrights, each paired with a carefully-chosen passage from *The Message: Catholic/Ecumenical Edition*, a fresh, faith-filled, contemporary translation of the Bible.

LOUISA MAY ALCOTT
HANS CHRISTIAN ANDERSEN
CHARLES DICKENS
ELIZABETH GASKELL
HERMAN MELVILLE
WILLIAM SHAKESPEARE
EDITH WHARTON

800-397-2282 ♦ ACTAPUBLICATIONS.COM